Burntisland Voices

Recorded Memories of Local Folk
1910-1970

Edited by Iain Sommerville

Published by Burntisland Heritage Trust
with financial assistance from the Heritage Lottery Fund

Project Managers

Ian Archibald   Helen Mabon   Iain Sommerville

Interviewers

Ian Archibald	Ian McLeod
John Burnett	Jill Potrykus
Hugh Fisher	Iain Sommerville
Bill Kirkhope	Jinti Wight-Boycott
Helen Mabon	John Wright

Transcriber

Vivienne Miller

Published in 2005 by Burntisland Heritage Trust
4 Kirkgate, Burntisland, Fife, KY3 9DB, Scotland

British Library Cataloguing-in-Publication Data:
A catalogue record of this book is available from the British Library.

ISBN 0-9539353-2-9

Designed by Iain Sommerville.
Printed in Scotland by Thos McGilvray & Son Ltd, Wemyss Road, Dysart, Fife, KY1 2XZ.

~ ~ ~ ~ ~

Burntisland Heritage Trust

The seal of the Royal Burgh of Burntisland

~ ~ ~ ~ ~

Cover Illustrations

Front cover: A street party in Dick Crescent, Burntisland, around 1947. James and Neil Ewan collection.

Back cover: Jimmy Wilson at the Binn Village, taken just after the end of the Second World War. The baby is Alex Hood, grandson of George Hood. George was the Binn Village's last inhabitant, departing in 1954. Jimmy Wilson collection.

'Princess Chrysanthemum' was a popular operetta in the first quarter of the twentieth century. Around 1913, it formed the basis for one of the Burntisland kinderspiels which are remembered in this book. The photograph shows May Wallace, who was one of the Princess's attendants in that kinderspiel. May later married Walter Carstairs, whose reminiscences are also included in the book. She received the Burntisland Community Award in 1983, in recognition of her voluntary work.
Iain Sommerville collection.

Contents

The Interviewees

The photographs in this section are from a variety of periods.

Janet Agnew (née Roy)

Born in Burntisland in 1929. Pictured in her Scottish Girls' Training Corps uniform around 1946.

Bill Cook

Aged 77 when interviewed in April 2005. Worked at the railway Control in Forth Place.

Jim Calder

Born in Bathgate in 1916. Worked at the railway Control in Forth Place.

Jim Cowie

Born in Kirkcaldy in 1939. Served for many years as a police officer in Burntisland, where he still lives.

Jean Carabine (née McKenzie)

Aged 90 when interviewed in April 2005. Born in Edinburgh. Family moved to the Binn Village when she was about eight years old.

Isa Duncanson (née Duncan)

Born at Burnside, Burntisland, in 1929. Has served as Secretary of the Highland Games Committee for almost 60 years.

Walter Carstairs (1904-1996)

Born in Edinburgh. Holidayed at the Binn Village. Married May Wallace and settled in Burntisland.

Sadie Edwards (née Roe)

Born in Burntisland in 1930. Pictured outside the old swimming pool in the late 1940s.

Annie Christie

Born at the Binn Village in 1922. Pictured at the Rev John Allan's Robing Ceremony in 1998, when she presented him with his robes on behalf of the Erskine Church.

Albert Gunn

Born in Burntisland in 1924. In December 1943, during the Second World War, the engines of his bomber failed over Germany. He parachuted to safety and was taken prisoner.

Jim Harvey

Born at Duncrievie, Glenfarg, in 1919. Came to Burntisland when he was six months old. Ran his own joinery business in the town.

Norman Balfour Mackie

Born in Burntisland in 1913. Closely involved with Burntisland's cinemas and the Parish Church.

Violet McFarlane (née Muir)

Aged 91 when interviewed in March 2005. Lived in Burntisland until her marriage in 1938.

Rolf Rademacher

Born in Wuppartal, Germany, in 1926. Taken prisoner in the Second World War. Settled in Scotland, and has lived in Burntisland for 50 years.

Cherry Rigby (née Reid)

Born at 2 Buccleuch Place, Burntisland, in 1921. Served in the Dental Corps in the Second World War.

Bill Stratton

Born in Poland in 1916. Settled in Scotland after the Second World War. Shop proprietor in Burntisland for many years.

Betty Traynor (née McNeil)

Born in Paisley in 1917. Family moved to Burntisland when she was four years of age.

Cathie Watson (1904-1998)

Born and bred in Burntisland, where she lived all her life. Followed a career in teaching, becoming a headmistress.

Jimmy Wilson

Born in Leith in 1915. Lived at the Binn Village from 1922 to 1934. Served in North Africa and Italy in the Second World War. Trustee of Burntisland Heritage Trust.

This book contains copies of a number of items saved by the late Alex Mackinnon, who worked in Burntisland Shipyard. The old snapshot on the right shows Alex and his brother Willie in the High Street. Alex is on the left of the photo, which was taken in the late 1940s.

The Burntisland Shipyard Employees' Discussion Group

*Ian McLeod assembled the members of the Shipyard Employees'
Discussion Group for this photograph, which he took at
Burntisland Harbour and which has the old shipyard in the
background. From left to right are Johnston Wood, Tom Allan, Bob
Miller, Tom Lawrence, and Alex Ferguson. Unable to be present,
but captured later, was Bill Strawn - in the photograph on the right.
The group's reminiscences are recorded in Chapter 5.*

Tom Allan

Born in Burntisland in 1926.
Welder and latterly Quality
Control Inspector in the shipyard.

Alex Ferguson

Born in Burntisland in 1931.
Welder in the shipyard.

Tom Lawrence

Born at Seafield Farm[1] in the
Parish of Kinghorn in 1924.
Welder in the shipyard.

Bob Miller

Born in Burntisland in 1928.
Contracts Manager in the
shipyard.

Bill Strawn

Born in Rosyth in 1929.
Loftsman in the shipyard.

Johnston Wood

Born in Burntisland in 1930.
Manager of the shipyard.

---

[1] Tom was born in the ploughman's cottage, which was in the middle of one of the farm fields. He enjoys telling
people that he was "born in the middle of a field"! The cottage was demolished and buried many years ago.

Preface

Burntisland is a small resort town in Fife, Scotland. It is situated on the north side of the Forth estuary, opposite Edinburgh. Its population at the time of writing in 2005 is about 6,000.

For most of the twentieth century, Burntisland earned its living from a mixture of industry and tourism. In more recent years, like other towns in Scotland, it has had to adjust to changing industrial patterns and to the availability of inexpensive holidays abroad. The shipyard closed in 1969, and the aluminium works in 2002. Burntisland still plays host to holidaymakers and day trippers, but not in the numbers of former years.

So the town is changing, but there is much to remember from the experiences of the twentieth century. Some families make an effort to record the memories of their older members, but often this is not the case: many old folk leave us and take a small but irreplaceable part of Burntisland's heritage with them.

In 2004, Burntisland Heritage Trust decided it was time to do something about this gap in our local history, and the Burntisland Oral History Project was born.

The aim of the project is to record for posterity the reminiscences of the older folk in the town, and to make the recordings available to as wide an audience as possible.

To get things moving, we decided that a special initial effort was necessary. We therefore set ourselves the target of carrying out the first phase of recordings and producing a book based on these by mid 2005. We secured a grant of £4,467 from the Heritage Lottery Fund towards the costs of equipment, training, transcribing and printing. The grant conditions included a stipulation that the book should be completed by the end of July 2005.

This first phase of recordings was carried out by ten volunteers in the period February to May 2005. Twenty-four people were interviewed, some more than once and some (notably the shipyard employees) in groups. The principal content of this book comprises edited extracts from these interviews, and also extracts from two interviews which were fortuitously carried out by Helen Mabon in 1995.

The book is not intended to be in any way comprehensive. The contents are derived from what our interviewees talked about. Most of the people we interviewed were nominated at meetings of our volunteer interviewers, and the broad subject areas were also agreed at these meetings. But the approach was very flexible, and we did not attempt to impose a detailed master plan. Having said that, we hope that the book does give a good flavour of how Burntisland used to be - as related by those we interviewed, in their own words. The period covered is, broadly, 1910 to 1970.

We have reproduced what our interviewees told us. That is the nature of oral history. But we must bear in mind that memories are fallible!

We intend the Oral History Project to be a permanent feature of our activities, and to continue our programme of recording in the future - albeit at a less hectic pace. We also hope to make our original recordings and full transcripts available at Burntisland Heritage Centre and other public archives.

Finally, I am very grateful to all those who helped with the project. Their names are recorded on page 10. I should also like to add a special personal word of thanks to my fellow Trustees, Ian Archibald and Helen Mabon, for their outstanding contributions.

Iain Sommerville
Editor; Trustee, Burntisland Heritage Trust

Burntisland, June 2005

Acknowledgements

Many people were involved in this project, which was truly a team effort. Burntisland Heritage Trust record their sincere thanks to them all.

There would of course have been no project at all without the reminiscences of those whom we interviewed. Their names and photographs are on pages 6, 7 and 8. We thank them for their patience and tolerance, and we hope that they themselves derive some satisfaction from the fact that the Burntisland which they remember is now recorded for posterity.

Similarly, we could not have carried out the project without our volunteer interviewers. Their names are listed on the title page. In many ways it is more difficult to interview than to be interviewed, and we are grateful to our volunteers for their good natured commitment.

Our transcriber, Vivienne Miller, had what was often a difficult and demanding job. She produced remarkably accurate transcripts of the recordings, cheerfully and conscientiously.

The publication of this book was made possible through financial assistance from the Heritage Lottery Fund, who gave Burntisland Heritage Trust a grant of £4,467 for equipment, training, transcription and printing. We record our gratitude to them, and to the Glasgow office of their small grants organisation, Awards for All, who processed our application with maximum speed and minimum fuss.

There are more than 130 illustrations in this book. We are very grateful to the following people for allowing us to use their old photographs and documents - Janet Agnew, Alan Barker, the family of the late Walter Carstairs, David Robertson Collin, Isa Duncanson, Sadie Edwards, James and Neil Ewan, Albert Gunn, Bill Kirkhope, Dave Lawson, Norman Balfour Mackie, Iain Mackinnon, Linda Oldham, Cherry Rigby, Elaine and Gordon Ritchie, the family of J.L. Stevenson, Bill Stratton, Captain Henry Watson, and Jimmy Wilson. The source of each illustration is recorded with its caption.

Stewart Simpson's assistance in scanning photographs was much appreciated, as was Ian McLeod's in taking the photographs of the shipyard employees. John Burnett read drafts of the various chapters, and made many helpful suggestions.

Nancy Arvay assisted with the procurement of equipment. Elaine and Gordon Ritchie supplied useful additional material.

Valda Hood-Chin and her team provided training for the interviewers. Sandy Lobban helped us to unravel the mysteries of Hi-MD minidisc recorders.

George Milne and Teresa Henderson of our printers, Thos McGilvray & Son Ltd, gave us helpful advice on many occasions.

Notes for the Reader

The main question I had to address when assembling this book was the degree to which the interviewees' spoken words should be edited. On the one hand, I wanted to reproduce what was said, as closely as possible. On the other hand, the book had to be easy to read. This was not a problem peculiar to our book: professionals in the oral history field debate this subject frequently and vociferously. I was nevertheless somewhat taken aback when I read a book[2] by the highly respected Kintyre historian, Angus Martin, who had originally intended to produce a manuscript based on taped recordings of fishermen, using their spoken words transcribed precisely. He eventually gave up, commenting: "How many people will actually bother to read this stuff?" The final version of the book was virtually all in Angus Martin's own words - and was highly readable, of course!

I decided, however, that such drastic action was unnecessary with the material I had, and I hope the readers agree. Some editing was indeed necessary, notably the removal of extraneous material and the addition of words to assist comprehension - although the book remains essentially a true record of of the spoken words of the interviewees.

The following notes describe how changes are indicated in the text, and also explain other matters.

❖ Broadly speaking, the passages in italics (including captions) are text written by the Editor. The other text (except that in square brackets) comprises the words as spoken by the interviewees.

❖ Five dots (".....") indicate that words have been removed.

❖ Words in square brackets are clarifying additions made by the Editor. In some cases these represent the inclusion of the gist of an interviewer's preceding question.

❖ Five tildes (~ ~ ~ ~ ~) between paragraphs indicate that the paragraphs above and below are not directly connected.

❖ Each chapter has its own individually numbered series of footnotes.

❖ The date of an illustration is unknown if it is not stated.

❖ The source of each illustration is recorded with its caption. The exceptions are a few where the source is self evident. Where the source was the archives of Burntisland Heritage Trust, this is shown as 'BHT collection'.

I.S.

---

[2] Herring Fishermen of Kintyre and Ayrshire, Angus Martin, House of Lochar, 2002.

Chapter 1

Recreation and Entertainment

The Cinemas

As befitted a seaside resort town, Burntisland had a long and happy relationship with its three cinemas. The first was the Palace at the corner of Kirkgate and East Leven Street. It had a short life, a decade or so, and it closed in the 1920s. The main reason for its closure was the opening of the Porte Cinema around 1916. The shell of the Porte survives, a prominent reminder of one of Scotland's first purpose built cinemas. Grandest of all, the new Palace Cinema in the High Street superseded the Porte in 1939. It stopped showing films around the early 1970s, and was destroyed by fire in 1985. Its façade remains, albeit in a poor state of repair.

Norman Mackie describes his family's close involvement with Burntisland's three cinemas:

[My sister was] Anne Crammond Mackie, A.C. Mackie. She started off in the Palace in the Kirkgate, that was the Picture House, silent pictures, in the Palace which is right opposite the Parish Church gates, and in those days you had entertainment on a Friday and Saturday on the stage, and silent pictures. I have a picture of the picture house, of the Palace at the Kirkgate; and my sister started off as a projectionist and from there she rose to assistant manager to Mr Maxwell, who was manager; and when Mr Maxwell retired my sister was promoted to manageress; and then the company who had the picture house, they bought the cinema at the Porte in 1927. ..... The Kirkgate one must have been prior to the First World War. .....

Yu see we had another cinema going at the Porte, silent pictures also, but the Burntisland Associated Pictures ..... wanted to expand and they wanted a sort of modern building because the cinema, the Porte, was built as a picture house, although it's a queer building ..... and they decided to get down on to the High Street so that's why they acquired the cinema; and in 1928 they decided talking pictures were coming in so they installed talking pictures. It was the British Thomson-Houston Company who installed the first talking machines in the cinema in Burntisland.

And the Burntisland Associated Pictures wanted to move with the times and they decided to build a special picture house with all the modern techniques, and projection, and seating, and having all the benefits for the people of the town, comfort. In 1938 they applied to the Burntisland Town Council to build a picture house and two shops. This was granted in October 1938. The building commenced in December 1938. In October 1939, one month after the war [started], a new Palace picture house was opened on a Wednesday afternoon, and here was a beautiful picture house. ..... There were 200 seats in the balcony, and in the auditorium 800 seats. ..... So in all it seated about 1,040 persons. .....

The picture house opened during a very restive [time] during the war and although we had a few air raids apparently, I was away at the time, the picture house was open, it never closed.

Top left - the original Picture Palace at the corner of Kirkgate and East Leven Street (previously Burntisland's first Free Church); top right - the Porte Cinema; middle left - Miss Mackie in the lounge of the Palace Cinema in the High Street; middle right - the High Street with the Palace Cinema on the left of the picture; bottom - the interior of the Kirkgate cinema. Norman Mackie, Iain Sommerville and BHT collections.

And after the war the pictures become the focus point of Burntisland. Queues half way along the High Street at weekends and when any attractive picture was showing. The people from Kinghorn and Aberdour would come and see them ..... At one time they had a picture house at Aberdour which was closed and Kinghorn was closed and Burntisland was only competing with Kirkcaldy, but Kirkcaldy had seven picture houses.

Eventually the picture house had opposition when television came in and they were finding that people were buying televisions and staying at home and the 1970s was crucial for the Associated Pictures, ... the cost of heating was more than what they were drawing in for the numbers that were attending the picture house, therefore they decided to close in the 1970s.

When you walked into the foyer you had a kiosk on your right. In the centre of the foyer was the cash box and downstairs you had the seating for approximately 800 people. Beautifully furnished. Behind each seat was an ashtray. So there were over a thousand ashtrays in the picture house counting the 200 in the balcony. Now you had wonderful staff members, who had to after each show in the evening, had to check every ash tray in case of cigarettes burning. Now that was done every night until 1972 and it was after the picture house was sold, it was run by a gentleman from Dunfermline who thought he could make it a paying prospect but it only opened for a few months and then closed. It was 1985 when the vandals set alight the picture house. So it took vandals to burn the picture house down. .....

Going back to the foyer, on the left was this wonderful staircase and long glass windows with beautiful reindeers in lead. And the décor in the lounge, the panels had also reindeers painted on the panels and the beautiful carpet had matching basket chairs. Lloyd loom chairs. And there you were. A beautiful lounge with people either waiting to go in to the picture house or to have a seat before they went home, and this lovely view of curtains to match the décor made it a most beautiful picture house.

No double seats, but in the cinema at the Porte they had chummy seats. ..... We closed the Porte cinema after the new picture house opened.

We ran the cinema. It was a family affair, we all had to take our turn because you couldn't expect my sister to [do it all] without a break for sickness or holidays ..... the family, my late brother Jim and I, we being on the commercial side of the family, we had to learn how to run a picture house, how to order films, and use our knowledge of percentage films. The better the film the higher the percentage you had to pay. Then you had to deal with the Customs and Excise of course on the ticket. Then you had to be able to buy from travellers. Sweetie travellers, cigarette travellers in those days, ice cream, dealing with ice cream people and it was interesting. Although I did this over and above my own job. .....

I would reckon about 500 seats [in the Porte cinema.] There would be about 150 upstairs and the balance downstairs and there was just one long, I used to call it a close. ..... As far as I was concerned it was no more a picture house than fly in the air, once we had moved into a quality built picture house. .....

The projectionist in the cinema followed suit; each picture house closed, they moved on, and they had to learn new techniques, talking machines. When talking machines were introduced into cinemas it was a new way of life for projectionists and of course you had a chief projectionist, and an assistant and a spool boy or a spool girl rewinding a spool. So you had three or four people in a projection box. ..... [That] applied to the cinema at Burntisland Porte and the one in the High Street.

I had to learn in the case of breakdowns and that. What did you do? You had to be shown how to rejoin films and all this. A break in the film, but it never happened that I had to do it, but I knew what to do. This was part of your training as a manager. And I think the greatest thing is the meeting of the public, how to meet the public. In a cinema where you had some poor films you got a lot of abuse when they come out! And the management [of other cinemas] usually stayed away in the office. ..... people would come and say "That was an awful film to show tonight. You should be ashamed of yourself", and all this.

Oh it really improved, the time of a breakdown. The time got shorter and shorter. It used to be a long time before a breakdown was rectified but latterly when you become expert, the projectionist, it was just minutes, oh you got a few boos but we usually put on a record.

..... the picture house at the Kirkgate had a pianist and she was a regular pianist, a Miss Fraser, a Mrs Fraser I should say, and she was a wonderful pianist. And she could play all the time and when there was a change in the film such as the news you could have a horse race and she would play racing music on the piano and immediately there is a death and a funeral she could break into a slow .....

Wonderful. And she would have a bag of sweets at the end of the piano, Mrs Fraser, and never miss a note and pick a sweet out and in her mouth.

On a Friday evening in the [Kirkgate] Palace you had a drummer and a violinist extra and it was a singalong night. On a Friday night where they showed the film and it was called the 'bouncing ball' so that the audience could join in singing, and you followed the bouncing ball on the screen, and the music covered the tune that would be being played you see. So this was their entertainment for the weekend.

Now when we moved to the cinema in Burntisland in the Porte there was also a permanent pianist, a Mrs Kinnear, now she was the regular pianist and she was also very adept at switching the tunes to go with the films that were being played. It could be a 'cowboy' which takes in great races and galloping music until you had a serious film and sad .....

Ad when we introduced the new picture house we introduced a sweet kiosk, whereas [with] the previous two picture houses we had a sweet shop outside. The cinema at the Porte, a Miss Stocks supplied all the sweets and also at the Kirkgate where the sweet shop [was], and Low's in the High Street who opened specially on a Saturday night to half past eight so that the people going into the second house of the pictures could buy their sweets. But that was all done away with when we involved our own sweet shop in the picture house.

Janet Agnew and Sadie Edwards reminisce:

Janet Agnew: The picture house ..... it had three different pictures per week. Monday/Tuesday, Wednesday/Thursday then Friday/Saturday matinée and Saturday night.

Sadie Edwards: And it had two shows. Two shows every night. We had a commissionaire. He had a lovely brown suit.

Janet Agnew: Uniform with gold buttons, brass buttons.

Sadie Edwards: And a big brown hat.

Janet Agnew: Big hat. Very smart. He was a big, big man. And it was a beautiful picture house inside.

Sadie Edwards: Lovely. ..... can remember going to the old picture house.

Janet Agnew: And you used to go to Miss Stocks's and get your sweeties.

Sadie Edwards: See what she had on the penny tray. She used to have a tray of things, each thing cost a penny and she used to lift it out, and you pointed to what you wanted and you got that for a penny. Then you went across to the picture house.

Annie Christie:

Went to the pictures, a matinée on a Saturday. Had the pictures one night in the week; we got to the pictures, because the pictures changed. They were on for three nights, and then maybe a Saturday afternoon we went to the matinée. That was in the old picture house at the Porte. Then, of course, when the new picture house opened, we used to go there. But it was black and white when we went to the one at the Porte. Used to go in the front seat and your neck was stiff, looking up. Used to sit for as long as we could for our money.

[When we came out,] we'd go to the chip shop and have a penny plate of chips, and just go into the sitting room and sit and eat them there. We'd be making a bit o' a racket, and Mr Allan would just put his head over the sort o' board thing, and that was it. He never spoke, just looked at us, that was enough. ..... We used to have all this sauce and vinegar and everything on your chips. Then we would walk up the road, just, and that was our night out.

Albert Gunn:

We were given newsreels in the cinemas. The 'talkies' had come, of course, with the building of the cinema at the Porte, and, I can remember there, by the way, the first film, I can remember it, I'll always remember it. I think it was four pence in old money, four pence and sixpence, the posh seats were sixpence. But four pence, that was our target, and I managed to rake this four pence up and joined the queue. And literally was going up the steps at the front to the box, when they said the four penny seats are full, so I didn't get in. So I had to come back the next night and queue again. And I can remember that picture; it was 'King Kong'.

Betty Traynor:

I remember as a wee girl going to the Picture Palace at the top of the Kirkgate. They were all silent films with a pianist playing at the front of the screen. I still remember how thrilling all the films were with lots of chasing like the Keystone Cops and all a great laugh. I think it cost you a penny or tuppence to get in and you could also get in with bottles or jam jars. Later on during the war we all went up to Mr Dabb the minister's Penny Picture Pops in St. Columba's top church hall.

Before we were married Joe and I used to go up to the balcony when we went to the cinema at the Porte and I still have fond memories of going to Lizzie Valentine's wee sweetie shop up Rose Street for chocolates.

Cathie Watson:

Oh yes, I remember sitting in the back seat [of the cinema in the Kirkgate] and looking at the pictures. It was awfully steep looking down from Leven Street. The seats were all stepped up. And they were just like steps and you just sat on them. Like benches but part of the step. We saw Pearl White and Charlie Chaplin there. ..... Mrs Fraser, she was a grand pianist and she lived quite near. She lived ..... on the hill going up to the Parish church. .....

Yes [my father] was Burntisland born and bred. ..... He was the first born of ..... ten children. That's him there and his father was called James Cook Watson. He's got the baby on his knee you see, and they lived in the bottom of Cromwell Road. You know where the old cinema is? Well that was the site of their house and their garden. Before the cinema was built it was a house in line with all the other houses. It was a long garden.

Walter Carstairs:

I was very ..... friendly with the manager [of the original cinema in the Kirkgate.] Him and I were very [good] friends. ..... His mother owned the place, aye. Originally, it was owned by a man and woman, who had a bicycle shop on the High Street. I canna' remember their name. ..... Oh they were hard seats, they werena' cushioned seats or anything. And we used to get the back seat in the picture house.

Violet McFarlane:

Just went to the picture house up the Kirkgate. I can remember the lady who, back in those days it was a piano for music, and the lady was playing good style especially when the Indians were chasing around and it was really great. She was playing for all she was worth and she had a bag of sweets at the corner of the piano and she was busy playing and eating those sweets as well, at the same time. And that was really funny. I can remember our Jess, my sister and I used to talk about this and have a laugh about it after we grew up.

Dancing and Socials

For many years, locals and visitors alike gathered at the Palais de Danse in Manse Lane

"Where youth and pleasure meet
To chase the glowing hours with flying feet".

The Palais gave enjoyment to thousands. Although the building has now gone, the name lives on, with the Palais Steps providing a convenient short cut from the town centre to Manse Lane.

Janet Agnew and Sadie Edwards tell Ian Archibald and John Burnett of their experiences at the Palais:

Ian Archibald: When you left school, ... what did you do for entertainment?

Janet Agnew: Went dancing to the Palais. ..... Oh the Palais was great. All the women sort of sat on one side and the men on the other side, and you all knew the good dancers. You always knew the good dancers.

Ian Archibald: Can you take me through the procedure?

Janet Agnew: Oh, they would always come and say, they would *ask* you to dance, and be real gentlemen about you, with you, and then eventually, come the end of the dance, they would ask if they could see you home. And if you knew them well enough, you might go with them, if you didn't, you wouldn't. But it was fun.

Sadie Edwards: By the end, we didn't go the Palais at the end of the war, but there was still forces about.

Sadie Edwards: ..... there was soldiers and sailors; the Palais was very popular with the Naval, from Rosyth and Donibristle, which was the Fleet Air Arm. And we, both of us, we used to go up as volunteers on a Thursday night, ... so we had lots of sailor friends. It was the NAAFIs, like, it was the NAAFI canteen ..... But it was a Fleet Air Arm, and you had, you were stopped at the gate and you had to say that you were on duty in the canteen that night. We spent a lot of time up there, and the sailors spent a lot of time in Burntisland. Aberdour Palais was another .....

Janet Agnew: That was a good one.

Sadie Edwards: ..... very popular dance place.

Ian Archibald: What about the music?

Janet Agnew: Oh-ho!

Sadie Edwards: It was wonderful.

Janet Agnew: Very good.

Sadie Edwards: There were bands that, I mean, you usually had a five or six piece band, both at Aberdour and Burntisland. We would have, there'd be a trumpeter, and there was always a clarinet and a sax, drums, piano and there was usually a bass fiddle.

Ian Archibald: What about singers?

Sadie Edwards: Aye, occasionally.

Janet Agnew: I remember one local singer, Bobby Easson.

Sadie Edwards: Bobby used to go up. He played the drums at the interval.

Janet Agnew: And his favourite song was the Hawaiian War Chant.

Sadie Edwards: The Hawaiian War Chant.

Janet Agnew: By, he could sing it too! .....

John Burnett: I was gonna ask, what was the names o' the bands?

Janet Agnew: Frankie Smith; they came from Edinburgh, originally.

Sadie Edwards: Mm-hmm. But he employed local people. Bill McIntyre played for him, who was, don't know if you remember him, but Bill was, he played the violin *and* the clarinet. .....

Sadie Edwards: George Boreham, he played the drums.

Janet Agnew: That's right, and Arthur ..... Clough, did he not play the piano?

Sadie Edwards: Miller, the chap Miller ..... played the piano, and Mr Halliday, he played the big bass. .....

Janet Agnew: They were good times.

Sadie Edwards: Yes, they were wonderful dances. It was my life. ..... that's where I met my first husband. .....

Old advertisements for the Palais de Danse. BHT collection.

Annie Christie:

..... later on after I was in my twenties, we used to go to the dancing, of course, once we got a wee bit, we started going to the Palais to begin with. ..... Oh, it was mobbed, the Palais, it was packed.

..... when I went, it was a Miss Hutton [who owned the Palais]; she lived up Craigkennochie, and then a Mr Biggar took over. He came from Edinburgh and he used to get a lot of the big bands to come.

Well, the locals were Bill McIntyre; when I first went Bill McIntyre had the band wi' the Henderson brothers, and Arthur Clough played the piano at the time. And it was really good then. We enjoyed it. But there was busloads came from Cowdenbeath and Kirkcaldy to the Palais. ..... It was good, it was really, there was never any fights or anything like that at that time .....

It was just a great big hall and they'd fancy lights on the ceiling. When you came in the door, you went downstairs to get into the hall and you could see just a haze of smoke, blue haze.

..... you just had to roll up your coat and put it on the floor in the cloakroom. There was no ticket place at that time, but there was after that; there was a place and a woman in it that took your coats. But you just had to roll your coat up and put it on the floor in the cloakroom.

Cherry Rigby:

I stayed up in The Glebe and I ..... was working in the Palais; I was in the ladies' cloakroom, and that was the heyday. Well, it was, aw, it was a hub. It was a hub of activity. There was no two ways about it. There would be a queue from the Palais door right down Paddy Waddell's stairs, you know the stairs? Paddy Waddell's stairs down to the Porte to get into the Palais. And when the Burma burnt down in Kirkcaldy, it was even worse than that. And there's been, I've seen even fourteen buses for taking the people away at night. That would be from 1950 on. That was the heyday.

I was there the night Frankie Vaughan kicked, did his kick off the stage on the band. He had one shirt, one nylon shirt and Teen McGuire had to wash that shirt and dry it, before he could get on the stage. He fell off the stage, kicking. That was true.

They had some big bands ..... Harry Gold and his Pieces of Eight, and ..... Alec Welch and his Jazz Band. And Frankie Smith's Orchestra, fourteen piece orchestra. A thousand and odds [on a typical big night.] Actually, there was far too many people in, today it's a fire risk. It would never have been passed.Oh, it was happy days.

[Trouble only] now and again. It wasn't really too bad, it really wasn't. ..... There was always a lot o' sailors. I've seen three ..... buses, and asked where some of them went rather than go on the bus. ..... Oh, yes, there was a few [ladies of the night.] There was a few of them, aye.

Always said that after I retired I was gonna write my memoirs and they would be banned!

Jim Harvey:

And then, of course, you had the Palais at that time as well. Which was a very popular dance hall. There used to be busloads come from round about for a Friday and Saturday night. And I would say, at that time, that was one of the best businesses in the town.

..... it was decided we'd all go to the old-time dancing at the Palais. At that time, Frankie Smith's band was there and he had a seven piece band for you. So we went to the Palais, and my wife and I, out o' the company that went to the school, were the only two that kept going. And eventually, we fell into another circle of friends, ... Davie Taylor and his wife, and, aw, there was a whole host.

How much was the entrance? Two shillings. ..... A seven piece band, aye. ..... That was on a Monday night. .....

At that time, Mr Biggar, who had it, was in the Dance Association and there was big competitions took place in the Palais, at that time, old time competitions. And they came from all over; Aberdeen, Edinburgh, Glasgow, even from England up to it. And it was a big, big event. ..... And they also had big country dances in it, at that time.

It was occupied by soldiers during the war, aye, aye. So that was the start of my taking an interest in sequence dancing. I've been very much interested in sequence dancing ever since. .....

Making your own entertainment - a street party in Dick Crescent around 1947.
James and Neil Ewan collection.

The Episcopal School Dance Team.
Back row - Moira Birrell, Agnes Rae, Miss Burns, Margaret Fraser, Sadie Roe (now Edwards).
Front row - Janet Braid, Agnes Marshall, Janet Fraser, Jenny Carstairs.
Sadie Edwards collection.

Burntisland Silver Band in fancy dress, around 1939.
Back row - A. Brett, L. Wallace, C. Walker, A. Meldrum, G. Henderson, J. Johnston,
B. Meldrum, R. Doig, C. Terris, H. Green, (unknown).
Front row - D. Young, D. Duke, R. Wallace, G. Wishart, W. Brown, J. Duke.
BHT collection.

Burntisland Pipe Band in Rossend Terrace. Collection of the late Mrs Margaret Lawson.

Well, if you go back to just after the war, we had all our districts in Burntisland welcoming people home, and in due course, we all had our social activities for the different areas; the Kirkton area, the Castle area, the High Street and the east, they all had their social evening for people. .....

Well, it was a social evening with singing. There would be a sort o' a concert party for the first part of it and then there was dancing after that. No' the dancing that you get nowadays! ..... It was mostly in the church halls, St Andrew's church hall and our own church hall. The Memorial Hall was in big demand at that time. The majority went there because it was the biggest hall, and could accommodate them. Oh, you'd accommodate in atween one and two hundred people at these things. .....

The Memorial Hall in Burntisland was built in Mr Dabb's time. ..... The one furthest from the front hall is called the lecture hall, and then behind that you've got the minor halls, rooms 2, 3 and 4. Then behind that again, you've got the Memorial Hall ..... It's the biggest hall in Burntisland, actually .....

Jimmy Wilson:

Well, if it was light nights, you were playing football, or whatever, maybe, or night time you were going to the dancing. ..... on a Saturday night we used to go to Edinburgh to maybe watch a football match in the afternoon, then go to the dancing at night, in Picardy's or wherever it was the dancing that night, anywhere.

Sadie Edwards:

But with the early teens, my early memory is, my mother was a great card player. She went to whists and they had a hall up the Kirkgate called the NUR hall, which was the National Union of Railwaymen, and they had ..... a committee all for the railway people. But they ran whist and dances every Saturday night, and I used to go with my mother, like many other children of my age. And we used to sit by the fire while they had their game of cards. Now that was twenty-four hands, and we sat, and then when they were finished, they cleared it away and the band came in and then it was dancing. And all these old, well, these women and men used to teach us to dance. And that was how I learned to dance, at the NUR hall ..... Mrs Montgomery, who was an old, a beautiful dancer, Mrs Halligan, Mrs Anderson; they taught us all the dances. And from then on you graduated to dancing with the boys!

Isa Duncanson recalls the early days of her dancing classes:

..... I practiced every night at home. Then we had a wind-up gramophone and I had all the records. [Mum and dad] bought me all the records, I had them all, because it wasn't tapes in those days, it was a gramophone and that was what I had for the class in the house as well, when the girls, half dozen girls used to come and dance, that's what we used to do. .....

I've taught, I think, in every hall in Burntisland ..... At first when I started, I just did it in my parents' house. And ..... it wasn't a big house. We were at the Burnside and on a Friday night, mum and dad used to go to the pictures, and I used to have the children in, and they had great times in the house. There was people like Betty McCowat, Margaret Frew, two sisters McGillvray, and they all travelled from the High Binn down for their dancing lesson. But that was where I did it to begin with. And then ..... there was so many children, and I was in the St Serf's church hall, been in there, Unity Hall .....

The New Year

Norman Mackie:

Now I remember as a boy we used to take in the old year, the new year, outside the Town Council clock. I was taken down one old year's night and I always can remember when twelve o'clock approached; the Roundhouse bell went; the shipyard bell went; the town clock struck twelve; the aluminium horn went; the ships in the docks all blew their horn; and it was just a wonderful sound of various noises. ..... Better than fireworks, and everyone was sober. ..... A wonderful memory for me being taken to an old year's night to see the New Year in. To hear all these wonderful old sounds from all the industries in the town.

Swimming and the Old Pool

Sadie Edwards:

Yes, we got a pool built in, the original pool in Burntisland was built, '38? ..... I think it was 1938 it was built and it was a great 'hoo-ha', the opening day ..... everybody in the town was down on the opening day, and all dressed and waiting to get in the water. And we always went with our parents to that sort of thing. Well I would be eight then, and I was pushed in the water. I'd never been in a pool before but I was pushed in, and I couldn't swim, and I've been terrified of water ever since, and you can't get me in the water. But that was the opening day, because we were with the Gunn family, who was an old Burntisland family as well, and it was George Gunn, bless him, who pushed me in, and oh, he got such a row from his mother *and* my mother ..... that is one of my early memories as well, George pushing me in the pool.

Cherry Rigby:

..... Oh yes, swimming, that was my main hobby, really. ..... I was the first captain at the club and Jimmy ..... Robertson was the first men's captain. But we went to the, it was a barge. ..... it must have been at least six, seven years before the pool. That's where I learned to swim. In the sea, yes ..... No, I wasn't conscious of [the water being dirty] and if we didn't get to swim, if the tide was against us, we used to go and swim from the Black Rock. ..... We used to swim from the Black Rock into the barge. They were strong, we were all strong swimmers, but maybe no' technically correct .....

Cherry Rigby's certificate awarded by the Royal Life Saving Society in 1936.

24

Two views of the old swimming pool. Alan Barker collection.

Cathie Watson:

[The swimming pool was opened by Mrs Leith,] the Provost's wife. That's where I learnt to swim. Oh no I didn't, I learnt before that. The original thing was we had an old boat and they put spars across it to make it solid and we swam out to that. They had steps down from the edge of the quay and then you had to get out to this boat. So you had to learn to swim. That was the whole idea and there were ropes and you could catch the ropes you see. Nancy Simpson, she was my chum and she could swim, and she taught me to swim. She held my chin up. ..... So that was the sort of custom before the swimming pool was built. ..... That's how it started and that's why it was at that part of the prom because it was a very short prom when I was a girl. ..... [The pool] was a great asset and then of course they extended the promenade you see.

Annie Christie:

And there was swimmers from Cowdenbeath came down, and they were great swimmers, of course, and we used to watch them. Oh, we had great fun at the swimming pool. We had season tickets that we got, and we could go down every night. ..... I remember my pal, she says, "I'll hold your chin up if you hold mine up," so she got a shot and she said, "Right, you have a shot," and she musta' thought I was doing all right and let my chin go and I went under, so that was it, I never went back into the water. But before the swimming pool ....., there was a wee paddling pool in the beach, just a sort o' oblong thing at the tunnel and we used to paddle in there at nights. Go down in the summer, after the school and that, and paddle about in there.

Other Sports

Cathie Watson on golf, tennis, curling and other sports:

[My father played golf on the Links] originally, that's right. They were there at the very beginning of Dodhead. Ten children all together. That's right enough, and they all played. All the boys played on the Links. You see, daddy and his brothers. Living on Cromwell Road that was quite near the Links, that's where he started golf. He didn't do it for very long because it was in his time they made the golf club and bought the ground up at Dodhead. So his name is up, I think he was the first secretary. Oh yes he was very keen.

..... and in the middle of this field there was a little white house and that was called Dodhead and it was there for many many years in spite of the fact that golfers, people were allowed to walk through the golf course. There was a right of way, right through the middle of the golf course and it stretched from the north road almost to the Delves. It was an 18 hole course, they bought the ground. It was just when I was a girl, I was only 15 when my father died. On a Sunday afternoon that was a regular walk. Up the North Road and then cross by the golf course and then down by the Delves. That was a regular thing. And lots of other people did the same thing. Sunday afternoon was the day for walking out with your family .....

I was interested in playing tennis. And we had four tennis courts just across the road. I used to stay in Greenmount Road, [opposite the bowling green.] Well that was where I was brought up. I was 40 years in that house. My father bought it in 1909. I was born in 1904 in Grange Road and we came down here to Greenmount Road in 1909. It was called the Tarry Dykes because the wall wasn't properly finished at the top. It didn't have a nice coping. They just had slabs along the top, flat, and of course the slabs had to be kept firm, tarred, gummed or glued on to the top of the wall and the result was the wall was flat across the top and the boys, the wee boys, they used to be wild, and they would climb up and walk along the top of the wall, but over the wall were the tennis courts ..... I don't know what it had been before, it was just a piece of waste ground, but anyhow it'll be in the history of Burntisland when the tennis courts were opened, but all the ground was divided up and they had a bowling green.

And four tennis courts. Oh I was so glad when the tennis started up. I was seven when I played tennis first, got my tennis racket, and my mother said "You cannie carry a thing like that, that's heavy." .....

Oh yes, the beach tea room. That was where we bought our sweeties. I used to run down from the tennis court, my Auntie Leggat and I, if we were waiting for a set, you know you had to wait your turn. Great fights used to go on to who was going on next and if we had a long time to wait we ran down to the beach tea rooms. That was the nearest for sweeties and ice cream to come up the road with but we always bought sweeties, usually boilings or something, black striped balls and then we had to hurry up in case we missed our turn. .....

And I was one of the first to learn to play tennis and we had three courts in a row and there was an extra one later on when it became popular. Lots of boys and girls joined up. They opened another court in the corner. Part of the ground was kept and tarred for a curling pond. Just flat and it was tarred over and it had lights. They erected, they put wooden stanchions in with a sort of lantern on it. And they had a row of these lanterns and of course at night it was a lamp with a wick in it. And they flooded this. It was like a shallow basin really and of course when it was frosty it froze and they skated on it and the men curled. Played bowls in the summer and in the winter when it was very frosty they curled. I remember watching all the men in the moonlight and with the lights on. The lamps, oil lamps, on these posts.

It's not so frosty now but we used to have hard winters when it froze without any snow at all ..... they formed a curling club and I remember daddy was the secretary. He was in most of the things in Burntisland. He was a great sportsman. At Cullaloe and at the reservoir, well they used to go up there, it would freeze up there too and I remember them getting ..... a brake ..... and a horse, and they would go up there and curl. At Cullaloe long ago. So I never felt the cold, we had woollens, my mother knitted my own socks. She knitted my stockings. Yes, yes, and a gym costume and a blazer, a thick blazer, what did we call it? A reefer jacket we used to call them but oh no, we never seemed to feel the cold.

We were running about all over the place. Played tennis in the summer and badminton in the winter. We had a good badminton team. [We played badminton] in Somerville Street. I don't know what hall it would be now.

Walter Carstairs on golf on the Links:

Yes, [I remember golf on the Links.] Easy, five holes. ..... That was at my younger days. Before I joined in, before I went up to the big course. But, I could tell you where the holes were, there were five holes and the longest hole was where the steps that goes up to the Roundhouse, you know the big long steps, well that was the fifth, or something like that, hole. But it just zigzagged. Och, we played all places because it was long grass and you lost your ball and that was you finished.

Norman Mackie on rugby and curling:

My favourite sport was of course rugby and rugby commenced in 1928 in Burntisland and the club, the first playing pitch, was at Cotburn where the Cotburn houses are. That was the first rugby field. And then they moved down to Bentfield which is now Ramsay Crescent and Duncanson Drive and that's actually where the rugby finished approximately at the beginning of the war in 1940. I could tell a little about the rugby club which was interesting.

Burntisland Rugby club, there was about 35 members and run two fifteens and when war broke out the first fifteen they had 11 members enlisted in the services, either called up or volunteered. And after the war was finished out of 18 that eventually enlisted from the club, 11 gave their lives for their country. Now 11 members out of a small rugby club of 35, the rugby club could not carry on after this wonderful sacrifice they made. During the period 1931 to when I joined the rugby club in 1940 was the experience of my life. I enjoyed rugby ..... the camaraderie of it was wonderful .....

I played centre forward and I played on the wing and played stand-off. I managed in 1944 when serving in the RAF to be chosen for RAF Scotland and played the Royal Navy at Invergordon in January 1944 which was a great honour to me. We beat the navy which was wonderful. Actually we had five professionals playing for the RAF, from New Zealand.

We mainly played in Edinburgh. We played either Heriots seconds, Royal High seconds .....

Our nearest neighbours Dunfermline and Kirkcaldy were our local matches, and Howe of Fife, but most games were played in Edinburgh, in Barnton Park, Trinity and Musselburgh; all the really junior teams. A really exciting time. When you were a young man you could play rugby in Edinburgh, and then have a night out at the dancing. .....

Actually after the long life I've had I took a great interest in curling because as a boy they used to curl at Meadowfield and when we played rugby the curling club had an outdoor curling rink early, and this was built early 1900. Any rugby pictures that have been taken are just in front of the curling rink at Burntisland Recreation Club. Unfortunately we have no picture of the curling club rink. Although the Burntisland Curling Club, they curled at Dunearn Loch and Meadowfield in the winter when it was suitable, until they had the curling club at the Recreation Club built. .....

Now to eliminate going curling to Dunearn and that, they had there own local rink and when the temperatures had dropped they had about two inches of water over the outdoor curling and it just froze over and that was it ready for curling. .....

The curling club as I recall, and told by curlers, they went by horse and they had the little traps and they could go up to Dunearn House and then there's a road that leads right to the loch. And they had their own shed, with all their curling stones kept in the shed, so they didn't need to move their curling stones with them.

[The curling club] must have [disbanded] after the war. It just faded out because the last treasurer was John Adamson who played rugby with me and he knew as a boy I was interested in the curling club. The curling club was formed in 1888 and the first meeting was held in the Burntisland town chambers. But that was the one and only curling club meeting held outside a hotel that hadn't a licence. Curlers had to have a licence.

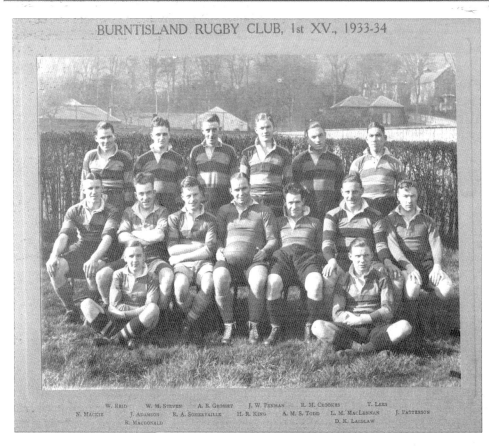

BURNTISLAND RUGBY CLUB, 1st XV., 1933-34

Burntisland Rugby Club 1st XV in season 1933-34. Norman Mackie is on the left of the middle row. Norman Mackie collection.

W. Reid   W. M. Steven   A. R. Grosset   J. W. Fenman   R. M. Crookes   T. Lees
N. Mackie   J. Adamson   R. A. Somervaille   H. R. King   A. M. S. Todd   L. M. MacLennan   J. Patterson
R. Macdonald   D. K. Laidlaw

Walking

Betty Traynor:

Walking was important to everyone before and during the war as nobody had cars and one of our favourites used be along the low road to Aberdour, to the Silver Sands. Quite often, there were two or three families of us and we had a picnic on the beach and walked back again in time for tea.

One of the most popular walks with families was along the beach to Pettycur, but if the tide was in, we would go along the railway embankment. In those days it seemed to be sunny all the time and we would stay there most of the day. Other times families would walk out to the Black rock and along the sandbank to Kinghorn and another good place for picnics was round the Lammerlaws.

The Delves was also an interesting walk and sometimes along the path right through the middle of the golf course and over to the Low Binn. Walking up the path to the Binn Village was rather a long walk and hard work and I remember as a wee girl going up there with my mother to visit friends. In those days there were plenty of families living there and there was a school and a wee shop and even a football pitch and it was a popular place for holidays for Edinburgh people.

Cathie Watson:

..... Oh yes. Everybody went for a walk [on a Sunday after church.] You went with your father and your mother. Sometimes Rossend Castle way. It was lovely to walk along the Monk's Walk to Queen Mary's bathing shelter. That's what they called it. I don't know whether it's still there or not but you pass Rossend Castle, along the Monk's Walk, by the coast, looking down, and at the very end there was this octagonal building and it had seats all round it inside and they called it Queen Mary's bathing shelter. That's what we knew it as anyway. I don't know whether it's still there or not. ..... Oh yes it was a great place. That was what we used to do on a Sunday. Go there or up the Binn. Everybody went for a walk on a Sunday afternoon. Oh yes and you could stand and have a chat [to the people you met.]

The Kinderspiels

Janet Agnew and Sadie Edwards remember the kinderspiels:

Janet Agnew: Well, I was in Mrs Brown's kinderspiel, which, we met up at the Parish Church as it is now, and I've got pictures taken of the children that went up there, and there were loads and loads of them. And we used to put on shows every year. I think the last one that I was in was 'Santa Claus in Japan'. And I'm sitting in the front and so is Sadie, and we're only about five or six, if we are that.

Ian Archibald: Where does the name 'kinderspiel' come from?

Janet Agnew: Well, it's a German word isn't it?

Sadie Edwards: It's, is it not just a gathering of children?

Janet Agnew: Yeah, but I mean my kids went to 'kindergarten' in Canada, so I figured it was 'kinder' 'spiel', children's talk, gathering, or whatever. I mean a 'spiel' is a talk, isn't it?

Ian Archibald: Yes. That's right. So, was the show in the Parish Church hall?

Janet Agnew: Yeah.

Sadie Edwards: But it was performed in the Music Hall. You woulda' rehearsed up there, but the performance was really in the Music Hall, then.

A kinderspiel - 'Santa Claus in Japan' - in the Music Hall, around the mid 1930s. Sadie Edwards (née Roe) is in the second row from the front, fourth from the left. Immediately behind her is Albert Gunn. Sadie Edwards collection.

Janet Agnew: And I think most of the children in town went to it.

Sadie Edwards: Well, we've had photographs ....., and I mean it's just, there must have been, over a hundred on this picture, about a hundred children from ..... all age groups.

Ian Archibald: And these shows, were they on for an evening or a week?

Janet Agnew: Just probably an evening, I don't really remember. But that Mrs Brown that ran that, was the mother of Robert Brown that I worked for, ... that Mrs Brown was the Brown of 'Brown and Gilmour'.

Pantomimes

Isa Duncanson:

..... Then, of course, ... I'd be fourteen, when I took this notion to put on this pantomime and to give the money to the Red Cross. So, I wrote this pantomime, and ..... mum and dad went out every Friday night to the pictures and I used to have ..... mainly girls from my class at high school, at Kirkcaldy High School, and we used to practice this pantomime. ..... so my Father said, "What is it you're doing?" So I said, "I'm going to put a pantomime on." "Where about?" I said, "I'm going to ask Mr Dabb, the minister, if he'll give me the Church Hall to do it." "He'll never do that!" my Father said, "And you'll have to pay for it." I said, "Well if I'm doing it for the Red Cross, I might not have to pay for it." .....

And I said, "Well I need to get tickets printed," and he said, "And who's going to pay for that?" "Well," I said, "I was going to ask you to do it, but you'll get your money back." "My money back?" he said, "Nobody will come." And I said, "Well, I think they will." .....

However, I convinced him and he got the tickets printed and we got three hundred and fifty tickets printed and that cost fourteen and eightpence, it's funny how you remember things. And we went out one night, the girls and I who were in it, and that was only a handful, and we went round the town and sold every ticket.

And then other people heard it was going to be happening, it was a Wednesday night in St Columba's Church Hall, and people were all wanting tickets, but there was no tickets left. And I can remember going, we had a dress rehearsal and I can remember when we went to go up to the hall, the queue was away down the Kirkgate

..... They were sitting everywhere, and it had a little raised bit at the back, at that time, the top hall, and the stage was at the other end to where it is now; footlights, everything. And we did this pantomime and it was a sell-out ..... so many people turned away, we had to do a repeat performance. And we did that, then the Red Cross got the two lots of money added together .....

So that was that one, and then I got the bug to do this, you see, that was 'Cinderella', and then I wrote another one, 'Babes in the Wood'. And I thought, now what am I going to do that for? So, I did that for the Welcome Home Fund. Now that was all our soldiers, airmen, sailors who were away, there was a fund and they were all to get a meal, and they all got a wallet, for I have Jack's, with five pound in it for when they came home, see. So I thought, I'm going to do something for this Welcome Home Fund. So, we did 'Babes in the Wood', and again it was sold out, absolutely sold out, did a repeat performance. And then after that I did another concert, a dancing display, I think, for the Welcome Home Fund. It ended up I gave a lot, a lot of money to the Welcome Home Fund.

Well, then, after the War finished, I did a concert every year for the old age pensioners' Christmas Treat Fund. I did that every year. And it was a Mr Ewan, Jimmy Ewan, who was in charge of that. I think he was their secretary, and it was old Provost Meldrum, he was their chairman, and I did that every year for many, many years. .....

Well, the pantomimes, of course there was clothing coupons when I had the pantomime and we used to, they were wonderful, really, and we used to buy yards and yards and yards of butter muslin, and one mum would take one big bale away, and she would dye it all, if I wanted yellow. Another mother would dye all the blue, and that's how we had costumes, made out of butter muslin. And sometimes, myself, at that time, I would possibly play, in the 'Cinderella' one, I made myself 'Cinderella', and there was mums all gave clothing coupons so's I could have the proper dress, and the person who was the Prince, who was a girl called Margaret Blyth at that time, who lived in the town, and she got a lovely suit made. And then maybe another pantomime, I would have the suit and somebody else would be the Princess, and this sort of thing. But the principals, there was always mums willing to give up their clothing coupons to get proper material. But you had a job, even, getting that. And then there was another lady who used to make most of the costumes. But I can still see my mum's back garden wi' all these yards and yards o' butter muslin hung out on the line to dry. It was all dyed, but they were beautiful, absolutely gorgeous. We were still able to get the little sequins you see, and things like that. It was wonderful what you could do.

Fun and Games

Annie Christie:

Course it was warmer then, it wisna' like the weather we get now. But we played a lot at the beach, and we played oot the road there at rounders and 'kick the can' and everything. Course there wisna' the traffic on the road then.

We used to, well it was a can; you had to see how far you could kick it. The boys would be against the girls, you see, and they [would] always win, of course, 'cause they could kick it further than we could kick it. Then we played at rounders against them as well. There was a whole gang o' us here, mind. But ..... sometimes we were up the Binn; we'd a' go hiking away up the Binn. We were never away fae the Binn really.

Betty Traynor:

My early recollections were that there were always lots of children playing in and around Somerville Street. It was a happy time playing all the children's games such as skipping, sketches, tig and leavoy etc.

Albert Gunn:

[Time out of school was spent] mainly playing in the street. That was really it, but of course in Leven Street, we had the wonderful thing. We had the railway and the station, and at that time, there was a, or there still is, I think, but it's been blocked off, a passageway which went down under the railway line and came out about where, I think, the Railway Club is now, somewhere like that. So, of course, that was one game, and of course the other one was literally going over the present bridge over the railway and down the wooden ramp, ... usually we all wore boots. You could make plenty noise and usually we were chased out of there, but that was really the area.

It's difficult to think of the games, but it was mainly, a lot of it I think we did was running, and no' running away or anything. But I can remember, for instance, when we moved into Rossend Gardens, the little greenery area is still there, a sort of triangular shaped thing. Now we would run round at nights, and this is in the winter time. You were out every night. If you stayed in at night your mother wondered what was wrong, there was something wrong.

Sunday School Picnics

Violet McFarlane:

We went to the Parish Church Sunday School, Jessie and I, we had a very nice teacher there. Dr Logan's wife was my teacher and all the nice old hymns we learned. And then we had Miss Hutton and Mistress Brown the lawyer put on kinderspeils in the Music Hall. And we dressed up for that.

Well, we always had our Sunday School picnic in the summer to Piper's Farm, Mr and Mrs Piper's farm at the Grange. And it was lovely, we marched up with the silver band in front of us. And horses and carts with the horses all decked up and decorated, and we got into the park and that was good fun. And there was racing, mothers' race and the young ones' race and there was prizes for that. And outside of the back gate of the field up at Piper's there was an ice cream van, we'll call it that, and you got your halfpenny cone, for we had money to spend. And then when it was time for the tea or the milk you got a bag with a Paris bun in it and another bun in it. You got two buns in it and that was really lovely. When it was all over and time to go home, we were at the front gate of the big house belonging to the Pipers, Mr and Mrs Piper, and they were handing out an apple or an orange or whatever, a piece of fruit on the way out. I think we marched down back home again to the length of the Kirkton or something. But that was a lovely time and that was our Sunday School picnic every summer.

The Summer Visitors

Betty Traynor:

I always thought Burntisland was aptly named the 'Playground of Fife'. Well, the visitors would come on trips in buses or trains in their thousands mostly on Sunday school picnics.

They came mostly from the West and the Edinburgh area and lots of miners' gala outings from Fife and Lanarkshire. They always had their races, games and picnics on the Links although sometimes if it was raining they would go into one of the halls in the town.

The fair ground was always a big attraction although the beach was ideal for the wee ones with their spades and pails. The motor boat trips round the Black Rock and the rowing boats were great fun. When the swimming pool was built just before the war, this also was very popular.

A lot of houses in the town used to take in visitors for a week or a fortnight at a time. Visitors would rent a room and either make their own meals or have them provided. This was a very popular way for the housewives to make a bit of extra money. The busiest part of the season was the Edinburgh and Glasgow Fair fortnights.

Cherry Rigby:

There wasn't a lot [of noise from the shows], not really, no, no. But then, they were only allowed a long weekend at Easter, that was for the Edinburgh people, and for the Glasgow people, one week in July. It was only a week they got [at the same time as the Highland Games.] ..... They had *one* week ..... Yes, that was in 1930 because we were still in Buccleuch Place up till 1937. .....

Yes, we let the [house in Buccleuch Place to summer visitors.] ..... only for a fortnight. ..... my Father would be away at summer camp, 'cause it was the Territorials he was in, ... and he was away for a fortnight and my mother and I moved into the washhouse!

Bill Stratton:

..... specially during the summertime. You know, we had a swimming pool, and ..... golf, in fact, Links, just putting and things, children's paddling pool and [there] was a lot to do, even after the season was over, like, even September, October, before the snow came or bad weather came, always buses coming to Burntisland and mostly they came on Sundays because there was a prohibition, in their own places. [They could] drink when they travelled, in the Ex-Servicemen's Club and all the pubs. I mean they were filled up with men and women ..... Burntisland had a good name all around, I mean, there was no problem whatsoever. We had the twelve councillors there and they looked after you, they came asked if you have anything to say, anything to do, can we help you and all that was really on hand all the time. The Provost came every day, practically, to me.

..... well the police had one occasion or two occasions maybe where, after midnight they said they were too rowdy, with accordions in the street and big song, about twenty, thirty men behind and walking back and forward, with 'I Belong to Glasgow', and a' different things, like. But I mean, that was all in good humour, was no fighting, anything like that. So there were some broken window glasses, I suppose, there was one threw somebody else's against it, and knocks, got one or two, twice, got a window broken and ..... I was very lucky.

Cathie Watson:

We were a good seaside resort and, you see, every summer as well as us having the District Nurse staying with us for good, year in year out, my mother had extra bedrooms and she let to people for summer holidays. ..... They brought their own food. They just paid for the bed and paid for the room. That's how we managed to exist till I was able to get a job as a teacher. But certainly it was a very busy place in the summer. 'William Muir', the ferry boat went back and forward regularly all the time and brought the [people] across. It was quite cheap. ..... And there were Sunday trains and there were no cars in those days so they just had to walk from the station, or walk from the ferry. The ferry was a great thing long ago. The 'William Muir' has done very well.

The Pierrots

A pierrot is a clown or comic singer, traditionally working in seaside resorts. In Burntisland, the term "the pierrots" seems to have been extended to embrace any troupe of entertainers. They were to be found performing on the beach and sometimes in the Music Hall (now the Young Community Hall).

Walter Carstairs:

There was a pierrot where the swimming pool was built. There was a pierrot group there. Collins Pierrots was the name, Collins Pierrots, and what we used to do, they came roond rattling their moneyboxes, and we would run roond to the other side. ..... We didna' have pennies in those days. I can remember, just vaguely remember, at the other end of the promenade there was another pierrot group went out to sea. You know what I mean, stood on stilts.

Mr. Fred Collins', BEACH PAVILION ENTERTAINERS, BURNTISLAND

Dalton Payne's Entertainers, Burntisland, 1925

Fred Collins' Beach Pavilion Entertainers (top) and Dalton Payne's Entertainers (bottom).
They were the two most familiar troupes of beach entertainers to visit Burntisland in the
summer season, and they enthralled locals and visitors alike for many years.
BHT collection.

*The beach around 1926. The railway is busy, and the Roundhouse
(railway engineering workshop) dominates the skyline.
Alan Barker collection.*

*Another view of the beach, this time looking east and dating from around 1949.
Alan Barker collection.*

There were many ways to keep the visitors entertained. One was the annual Miss Burntisland contest (above). Another was performances by Burntisland Pipe Band, pictured below in 1931. BHT collection.

Cathie Watson:

They were on the sands. Jack Payne's Pierrots. They erected a thing themselves. A stage and of course they were just in the open air. They improved that later on. Fred Collins was the first pierrots we had and then we had Jack Payne's. Yes, Dalton Payne was his name. Can't remember who they had after that but the original ones were on the sands quite near the tea rooms. And then eventually when the new prom was extended they went round there.

Albert Gunn:

I went to this slipway, which is still there, near the old pool, where they do water ski-ing from now. And that was where the swimming club operated, and they used to have races and all the rest of it, and I had been decked up in my little sailor's suit to go down there on a Sunday, and I slipped and went down on the green seaweed or whatever it was, and mucked the thing up. I can recall before the pool was built and we used to have the Pierrots there in the summer, it was all fenced off and they had seats in there, and everything. And we used to go there, but we didn't pay to get in because we were outside looking over the fence, but we could manage.

The Wireless

Albert Gunn:

..... we had the wireless ..... The reception, oh, compared to today, I mean, we thought it was fine, I suppose, at that time, but I can recall, I think it was about 1938, so I would be about 14, they broadcast a heavyweight boxing fight from America, and it was Joe Louis, who was the unstoppable champion at that time, and he fought a chap called Tommy Farr, a Welshman. And Farr, I think, if I remember correctly, he actually went the distance with him, which was quite a feat, although he lost. But, of course, we were up and with the time change this was about two o'clock in the morning, our time, that we were listening to, or trying to listen. And of course, houses in those days, you had no electricity. It was gas lit, and of course all the street lighting was gas, ... because Burntisland Town Council had a gas works in Thistle Street.

[The wireless] worked off a dry battery. It was a dry battery and an accumulator and, of course, the thing that was the problem, always, was the accumulator, because they had to be constantly recharged. And many's the time when one of us would be allocated, "Remember to pick up the accumulator," from, there used to be Mentiplay's in the High Street, Murray, an electrician, and they used to charge the accumulators. And of course, if on a Saturday you forgot to pick it up, meant there was no wireless that weekend.

The Highland Games

Isa Duncanson describes her long involvement with Burntisland Highland Games and the Crowning of the Summer Queen:

I really went on to the Highland Games Committee because when Leslie Stewart, who was a Burgh Chamberlain here, when he came here, he had come from Annan and Annan have a lovely 'Crowning of the Queen', a pageant, and he was very, very keen to do the same here. So he said to me, I had met him because Elspeth, his daughter, came to the dancing, that's how you meet people, and he said, "If I really try to do this in Burntisland, would you train the children, and we could maybe do it between us?" So I said yes, I would do that. But it was the Highland Games Committee at that time who were paying for the 'Crowning of the Queen' and everything; it was run by the Highland Games Committee.

So then, Mr Livingstone, who was then the Chieftain on the committee at the time, he said, "It would be wonderful if you came on the Games Committee," so I went on the Games Committee. And then the person they had as Secretary was going to be emigrating somewhere, so, I was very young, I was only about sixteen, seventeen, and they were looking for a Secretary for the Games. And we used to meet in the Porte Tearooms, I can still see it yet, and Mr Livingstone said, "You could be the Secretary, Isa," and I thought, "Oh deary me, I don't think so." "Oh, you would manage that fine," he said. So there was I, appointed Secretary of the Highland Games and I remember going home in a dreadful state and saying to my mum and dad,

"Oh, do you know what's happened? But I'll never ever be able to do it!" And I remember mum saying, "There's no such thing as 'You *won't* be able to do it'. If it's something you want to do, you'll manage to do it," and they were always behind me. And I've been Secretary ever since! That's a long, long time.

..... Well, you really organise [the Games]. You take all the entries and when you have your committee meetings, you have to draw up your list of events and nowadays we've a very, very good handicapper, and he takes all the racing entries and then he handicaps everybody, and that all comes and it gets printed in the programme. And the most difficult thing nowadays, is sponsorships, because it costs such a lot of money.

..... One of the little girls who's coming [this year], her grandma had danced at Burntisland Games years ago, and she is just so thrilled that she's going to dance at Burntisland Games. And it's a super day, because it's a time when a lot of people who have emigrated come home, and they come and speak to you and, great, it's just really great. And I really feel very strongly about the Games because that is our tradition. .....

The Highland Games [Committee], they sponsored [the Crowning of the Queen], if you like, to put it that way; they paid for it. They always had a [separate] 'Crowning of the Queen' day, which in those days was called 'Children's Day'. There were twenty-eight children in it. You had a Queen, and you had a First and Second Maid to the Queen, and you had seven other Maids of Honour.

Now they were all big girls, sixteen, fifteen, sixteen, lovely tall girls. And what we did was, to get them dressed, was we asked people in the town if they had any, if they had a wedding dress they didn't want, and they were all dressed in long white dresses. And then we had the robes that we use today, and they have all the ermine fur on them and everything. They're lovely; they were gifted to us. And we had the crown made and it's a lovely crown. So that was ten girls in that. There were eight, eight little girls. We had six little Flower Girls and two Trainbearers. There were, now what have we got to, we've got ten big girls and we've got eight little girls, this is eighteen; so we had a First Lord and a Second Lord and we had the other boys, we had a Crown Bearer, Sceptre Bearer and six Heralds. That's what we had, and all those, all the boys costumes, ... they were all hired for they came with the velvet breeches and everything, oh, the proper thing. It was quite a thing. *And*, the lovely bit about it was, when I think of it, we had six huge black cars, like what are the big funeral cars now; we had six of them. So it was really done in style. And it went on for quite a lot of years like that. And we always had a titled person, somebody really important to crown the Queen. .....

It was a long ceremony; it was quite long. The Queen's speech was even quite long. The 'Royal Proclamation' by the First Lord, it was very, very long, and the whole ceremony, I think, lasted about three quarters of an hour at that time. It was really something. It was really lovely.

..... crowds of people use to come in to see it, busloads, busloads o' people. The Links used to be covered with people. It was really lovely. I enjoyed doing that; it was nice. ...... every child got a bottle of juice and a bag, a bag of cakes and buns. And that's why it was called 'Children's Day' and we used to sit in the NUR hall up the Kirkgate and we used to give out tickets. People came for their tickets for Children's Day. And children got it from the age of three to fifteen, and they all got their tickets. No, it didn't cost them anything. So it just got, it was just becoming too expensive, so then it stopped for a few years and then we thought we would resurrect it and start it up again. The last girl to be crowned in *that*manner was Wilma Gilbertson. She was the last one, and my Mum crowned her. They asked Mum to crown her, which she was thrilled at doing.

..... it's not the same and it's not done on that scale now, and it couldn't be. Nobody could ever pay for that now, 'cause it must have cost a lot of money, but that was what we did.

Above: Jeannette Dey is the Summer Queen in the second year in which the event was held. Her Flower Girls are: <u>back row</u>, from left, Wilma Hay, Agnes Williamson, Elizabeth Bruce, Shona Wallace; <u>front row</u>, from left, Fay Archibald, June Bolam, Irene Rigby, Dorothy Clarkson. Isa Duncanson collection.

Below: a Summer Queen and her full retinue grace the stage of the Music Hall. Isa Duncanson collection.

A Summer Queen with her attendants, including an alert military guard of honour.
Isa Duncanson collection.

..... We used to go to the cinema at night, and the kids were all in a big row, I've got photos of this, on the stage at that cinema in Burntisland, and whoever had crowned the Queen, we had entertained them to tea, and they stayed on and they did the presentation to all the children. And on that day, they all got a silver medal, a real silver medal, inscribed on the back with their name and the year and what they were, and a little chain. They all got a medal, which was rather nice. And the Queen, she got her medal, but she [also] got a big colour portrait of herself. There'll be a few girls in the town'll have that.

Walter Carstairs:

See I was in the Highland Games Committee at that time. Oh, not for the guinea, mind, but I can remember the old greasy pole going up, up against the railway and tied by ropes to the railway. ..... And then it was all, it was greased, eugh! And then we'd climb that pole in turn; the ham was on top ..... And we climbed up there. And then the kids, all were racing in the road. Many a time I've an awfy kick or a bump trying to catch the first one. You know how you used to run with the first one.

Bill Stratton:

..... I mean they came to the swimming pool for the Gala Day, on the Links, with a band, the pipe band, Burntisland Pipe Band was there and of course the Colliery Band from Lochore, was a big band from Lochgelly, miners' band. Oh there was a lot of music going on and entertainment and, of course, the Highland dancing as well. Glencraig had about 2,000 miners, and each family had children. I mean there was loads of buses, ten, twelve buses came ..... from Glencraig to Burntisland Links for Gala Day. It was a big do for them. They were running 100 metres, 50 metres, and they went to the swimming pool and, oh, ... the day was theirs, really enjoyable.

A Wee Refreshment

Retired police officer Jim Cowie tells Ian Archibald about a few local difficulties:

Jim Cowie: Oh, well, weekends became very busy at that time, in the early '60s, before the advent of the Forth Road Bridge, and before discos became the fashion. Burntisland was one of the main sources of attraction for weekend entertainment; the pubs, the hotels, and, of course, the Palais dance hall, the Palais de Danse. Friday, Saturday and Sunday night went ding-dong. It was busy.

The George Hotel, the Royal Hotel and the Crown were about the main sources of any problems, but the George, the George in particular .....

Ian Archibald: Where is the George about? .....

Jim Cowie: The George is renamed the Smugglers. ..... And the rear lounge was like an ice cream parlour, the way the seats were set out. The band were on a stage about six foot high, and there was a bar in the corner that, when any problems arose, snapped down, pronto! Nan Gunn was the barmaid there, and she could certainly handle them. And then you'd be sitting, having your meal break in the office; the phone would go, fight at the George. Of course, we're all in our twenties as well, the constables, and it was a race to get round there first! And invariably, the Navy, the sailors from HMS Cochrane, yes, Cochrane was based at Donibristle then, and so Burntisland was a favourite port of call for them. And there was many, many a punch up between the Navy and the locals and the outsiders from Cowdenbeath, Kelty and all. .....

Ian Archibald: So, what did you do with the miscreants, once you'd sorted out the trouble?

Jim Cowie: Well, really depending upon the severity of it. They were either bailed out, as we could bail them out, on police bail to appear at the Burgh Court, at the next monthly hearing, or if it was serious enough, they would be remanded in custody for a court, either on Saturday morning, or on the Monday. .....

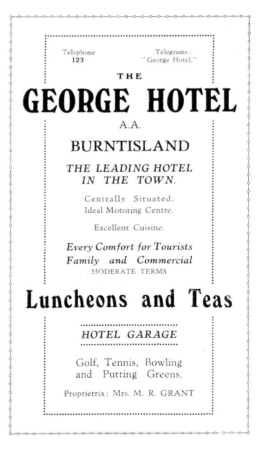

A George Hotel advertisement. BHT collection.

Jim Cowie: Well, I think about Burntisland, in itself, the winter months were quite quiet, apart from the, as I've spoken about, the fun and games at the weekend. Hundreds came into the hotels and the pubs, and the dance hall. But during the summer, of course, when the fairground was here, thousands upon thousands of visitors came to Burntisland. And then the annual Games Day, and that was an early start and a late, late finish. ..... in the early '60s, I suppose, for many, a visit to Burntisland Games Day, was the one day, the one day a year. ..... Burntisland was a great source of attraction for visitors from pubs and clubs and hotels, particularly in central Scotland and west Scotland and that. A day trip here on a bus, and the drinks and the fairground and fancy hats and Burntisland rock and they'd go back and start saving up for the next year. .....

Oh, yes, a multitude of buses. In fact, there was a bye-law brought in to govern the times when buses could come into and had to leave the town. ..... that came in about '67 or '68. ..... it only applied to the car park, the Links car park. Then by the Police Further Powers Act, we extended it to the whole of the Burgh. Oh, I've seen some bloody barneys there, going into the car park and there's several busloads going at it hammer and tongs and you'd pile out and get them on, escort them the other side of Aberdour or wherever, and leave them to it. They could sort themselves out after that. We werena interested who was on which bus or that!

The Links, packed to overflowing during the summer. BHT collection.

Janet Agnew and Sadie Edwards tell Ian Archibald and John Burnett about their experiences:

Ian Archibald: ..... were you aware of, you say you went to dances, was there ever any trouble?

Janet Agnew: Not really.

Sadie Edwards: No.

Janet Agnew: Not the trouble that they get nowadays anyway.

Sadie Edwards: Because they didn't have drink.

Janet Agnew: We weren't allowed to take drink.

Sadie Edwards: I mean there was no bars. ..... the boys that went for drinks, came in when

43

the pubs closed. Now the dancing was always quiet, fine, and it was the ones that were interested in dances were there. But there was always the element that had to go and have a drink first, and there was a few fights.

Janet Agnew: Oh, yes.

Sadie Edwards: Oh, people used to say, "Oh, some fight at the Palais last night!" and I'd say, "Well I was at the Palais, I didnae see any fight." No, but it was in the gents' toilet, but no great disruption to the dancing. It either happened in the gents' toilet or outside, but there was never, I can't recall once ever seeing any great disturbance.

Janet Agnew: Nope, neither do I.

Ian Archibald: Can you just tell me how many pubs you counted? .....

Sadie Edwards: I'm sure I counted fourteen at one time. Aye, I never went. It was a novelty if you went drinking.

Janet Agnew: That's right.

Sadie Edwards: And girls didn't go drinking.

Janet Agnew: We just didn't go into pubs.

Sadie Edwards: We didn't go drinking. I mean you didn't do it. It was older people and the boys that wanted to drink, went drinking. But the pubs closed at half past nine, ten o'clock, so they got to dance from ten till twelve. One o'clock, actually, I think, the Palais went on till on a Friday night.

Cherry Rigby:

'Sodger' Law. Yes, 'Sodger' had found a barrel o' rum from the Campania[1] in the 'Dead Man's Corner'. ..... Yes, before my time. It was my Grandfather that told me. At the breakwater leading into the Lammerlaws. That, where a prevailing wind, ... well that was the 'Dead Man's Corner'. So 'Sodger' Law found the barrel o' rum. He got absolutely, stociously drunk, and he kept going back to top it up until they found him, paralytic, utterly paralytic. So they put him on a barrow and wheeled him up to the gas works, where the retorts was, the retorts, gas retorts. ..... You see I knew it was a retort, because my Uncle Billy built them. And so they took him up there and he lay for *three days* until he sobered up .....

..... Oh, 'Watery Meg', oh yes! 'Watery Meg', Meg Mitchell. And she opened and shut her pub just at her own discretion. That was up the Kirkgate. 'Watery Meg', but that was true and she did. Yes, up the Kirkgate. Yes, she ..... actually she stayed along Kinghorn Road, there; the end of Buccleuch Place .....

---

[1] The Campania sank off Burntisland in 1918.

Chapter 2

Shopkeepers and Traders

Janet Agnew and Sadie Edwards recall the local shops:

Sadie Edwards: My first job was with Anderson, the newsagent. Alastair Anderson is our local electrician; well, I worked for his father from I was fourteen till I was nineteen, and he had the local printer's office. ..... It was a great business. He did all the printing for the local council etc. ..... Rankine's was another newsagent's. Now a Mr Brown bought it over and he hadn't a clue about newsagents, so he came to me, on the side, and asked me if I would like to go and work for him. I said, oh, I didn't know, you know, at nineteen ..... He said, "What do you, what's your pay here?" I was getting twelve and six a week. He says, "Well, I'll give you a pound if you'll come and work for me", so I agreed and I was so excited at this thought of getting a pound a week. Meanwhile, I'm working my week's notice, when Mr Forbes, McCrae Forbes, who was a customer of ours, came in and he said, "I believe you're leaving, Sadie." He was a wonderful old gentleman. I said, "Yes, I'm going to work for Mr Brown." "I didn't know," he says, "Would you not like to come and work for me?" I says, "Oh." "How much is Mr Brown paying you?" I said, "I'm getting a pound." He says, "I'll give you twenty-five shillings." I said, "I'll have to think about it." So I went to see my mother who was washing dishes in a restaurant in the town; she took, did all sorts of jobs, and I went along, I said, "Mr Forbes, the jeweller's been in and asked me to go and work for him. I don't know what to do." "Well, you just do it!" She was in agreement. But I had to go and tell Mr Brown that I'm sorry, I'm not coming to work for you. ..... I didn't like doing it at all.

Janet Agnew: Well, I lived, you know where the, what's the name of the shop that's where Robert Brown was? BURNTRA, you know the BURNTRA shop[1]. Well, that was Robert Brown the photographer; wireless sets, charged accumulators. Central Radio Service, it was called. Anyway, there was a lady worked for them, and she was drafted into the WAAFs. So I wasn't fourteen yet, so he came and asked if I could go and work part-time for them, which I did, and I got an exemption from school. But I had to go to night school for three years, because I got the exemption, which I hated, night school, for English, short-hand and typing. .....

Sadie Edwards: The old shops? They were all so individual, you know, the only company shops was Hay and Company .....

Janet Agnew: William Low.

Sadie Edwards: That was the only two company shops.

Janet Agnew: Ah-ha, Buttercup.

Sadie Edwards: Which are both grocers, oh and there was the Buttercup.

Janet Agnew: There was the Buttercup and the Beehive. The Beehive was a tremendous shop. It was wooden floors that you walked along, and they sold threads and buttons.

Sadie Edwards: It was an old fashioned drapers, and it had clothes right up to the ceiling. .....

---

[1] Now Harry's Cabs.

Janet Agnew: And the other one that was fantastic was Pittilo's. It was a hardware store. It sold everything from nuts and bolts .....

Sadie Edwards: He was next door to McCrae Forbes.

Janet Agnew: Yeah. Lots of *good* shops. How many shoe shops were there? Three, two, three counting the Co-op.

Sadie Edwards: There was the Co-operative. There was Woodrow.

Janet Agnew: Carr's

Janet Agnew: And about three or four chemists .....

Sadie Edwards: Three chemists.

Janet Agnew: And butchers.

Sadie Edwards: Five butchers. .....

Janet Agnew: You got, everything you could get in Burntisland; you didn't have to go anywhere else. .....

Janet Agnew: Or the van came to the door.

Sadie Edwards: Yes, we had loads of vans from the Co-operative, and the local butchers, they each had a van. Graham's had a van, Brown had a van, Cameron had a van. ..... And the Co-operative, and they also had horse and carts, baker's vans; they went all round the town. ..... And the gasworks, we had our own gasworks, but we had Mr Harvey, the joiner, Mr Brooks, the joiner, Mr Martin, the joiner, and they were all undertakers as well. That is who you went to when somebody died. ..... And Dewar, the joiner.

Janet Agnew: There was a fishery place as well, fishery place, over by the slaughterhouse.

Sadie Edwards: Aye, Drummond's, fish shop. ..... they used to smoke their own fish, on your road to the swimming pool.

Janet Agnew: And that wee fish shop in the High Street was lovely. It used to have running water coming down the window all the time. .....

Sadie Edwards: And we had Mr Crow, the plumber, Mr Reekie, the plumber, Mr Dunnet, the plumber. These were all one-man businesses, who would hire an apprentice, you know, and he would serve his time. They all had apprentices. ..... Mr Reekie's premises was where Allan Court is now, you went up the pend. His plumbing business was in there.

Janet Agnew: Mr Dunnet's was round in Rose Street.

Sadie Edwards: ..... Mr Martin was behind where that Fashion Flow shop was, the archway, I mean that's still there. Mr Murray the electrician had a shop on the High Street. ..... and there was a stonemason. Now, what was his name? A wee man, I can see him. Oh, what was his *name*?

Janet Agnew: We also had the shoe repair.

Sadie Edwards: He was a *wee* man.

Janet Agnew: And he was called 'the snab'.

Sadie Edwards: Aye, 'the snab'.

Janet Agnew: And we had ..... Blind Geordie's shop. And he had a sweetie shop, and he was blind, but he always knew when you went into that shop, because the step down had a crick in it.

Sadie Edwards: Had a bell.

Janet Agnew: Well, it did have a bell, but sometimes it wouldn't work and it had a wee crick in it.

Sadie Edwards: You went down two steps.

Janet Agnew: And he always knew when there was somebody in the shop. But he always sold you the right amount of sweets.

Sadie Edwards: He knew where everything was.

Janet Agnew: It was in the High Street. Now where was it next to?

Sadie Edwards: Next to where the Silver Tassie is.

Janet Agnew: That's right.

Sadie Edwards: Just down from where the new block of flats are. That's where Blind Geordie's was. Geordie Johnson.

Janet Agnew: And nobody ever tried to fiddle him!

Two old views of Burntisland High Street. Alan Barker and BHT collections.

TELEPHONE : **83**

Betty Currie

13
CROMWELL ROAD
BURNTISLAND

Hairdressing Salon
& Beauty Parlor

SHINGLING
MARCEL WAVING
MANICURE
FACE MASSAGE
ALL KINDS OF
ELECTRICAL
TREATMENTS

Select stock of Toilet Requisites

Established 1845.   Telephone : 44.

ROBERT BROWN

Meat Purveyor

High Street, Burntisland

**FINEST QUALITY HOME FED
BEEF, MUTTON, PORK.**

Pickled Tongues, Salt Rounds

Specialities :
COOKED MEATS OF EVERY DESCRIPTION
MADE ON THE PREMISES.

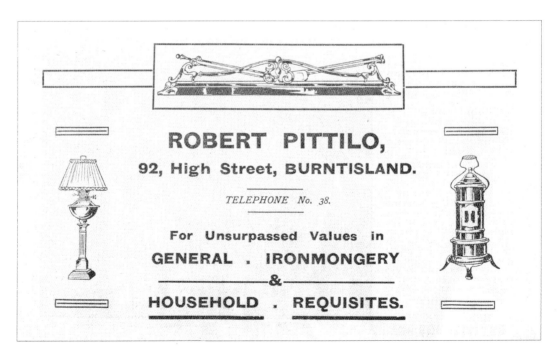

ROBERT PITTILO,
92, High Street, BURNTISLAND.

TELEPHONE No. 38.

For Unsurpassed Values in
GENERAL . IRONMONGERY
&
HOUSEHOLD . REQUISITES.

---

*On this page and the opposite page - some examples of the ways in which old
Burntisland businesses promoted themselves. BHT collection.*

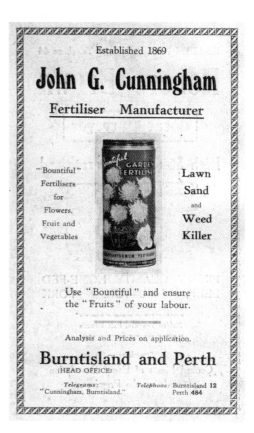

Albert Gunn:

..... thinking of money, money was very tight, obviously, for everybody. There had been a lot of unemployment in the thirties and, like most boys, you got a paper round. I mean there was loads of shops, and I got a paper round with the posh shop in Burntisland, that was Wood's the stationers. Wood's was a large shop, now it's John Cooper's amusement arcade. And we did very well, because, it's strange how you remember things, I had nineteen papers to deliver in the morning and three at night. It's amazing how you remember, you know, these silly things.

And, of course, what you had to do, which is different from modern times, all the boys had to go up to the station in the morning about half past six and get the early train coming down from Dundee with the Courier, and, of course, the train coming from Edinburgh and Glasgow with all the other papers. And Wood's, we had quite a big barrow with quite big wheels, I should think they were about four foot diameter, with steel rims, and a lot of the Kirkgate, at that time, was cobbled, in parts, so you could imagine in the morning, us hurtling down the hill.

There were all sorts of complaints about the paperboys, but the rush was to be first down the hill with the papers, and there was all sorts of nonsense went on, because the train would come in and the guard on the train would just chuck everything out onto the platform, so it was a free-for-all. And, of course, if you picked up one of the other lot's papers you hid it somewhere else, you know, and this sort of thing, until you got your own. And, of course, the others were doing exactly the same. But it was all good fun.

So I did that round, and I can still recall the three papers I delivered, and I used to deliver to Brown, the butcher, that's the one where Brown and Gilmour's shop is now. I then went to the Manse, the Parish Church Manse, which was in Cromwell Road at that time, which is now Grayforth House and delivered to Mr Dabb. And then to Rossend Avenue, as it was in those days, it's now Broomhill Avenue and a paper for Mr Martin the joiner. And that was it. ..... that was the three evening papers.

But where I got, not caught, but where I had to do my bit, was Wood's, they were the ones who stocked all the, shall we say, more expensive magazines and that, monthly magazines. So once a month, you had a load to deal with, but it was all good fun and there it was. And I was paid, that was a morning/evening delivery and I was paid two shillings and sixpence. 2s 6d a week, that was a Monday to Saturday, no Sunday papers.

..... And there were very few boys or girls who went on to Kirkcaldy. Obviously, when I say the 'chosen few' I'm being quite complimentary there, because they were obviously the brightest ones. I don't think I worked as hard as I should have done ..... However, the one thing we were looking for, "Let's get away from school." So I was still 14 in 1939 when the war started, and we all left school in July, looking for jobs. I had switched from being a paperboy to being a roll boy, and that meant that I was working at Ferguson, the baker's, delivering the morning rolls.

And I did the High Street area, and there's, I mean, obviously, you've got quite a number of buildings, three floors and so on, and we became quite expert, because you went out with a basket of rolls, piping hot, out of the oven, into bags, and you would drop them at people's doors at half past six and quarter to seven in the morning, so they could have them for breakfast, or they would make them up for the man's piece at lunchtime, if he wasn't coming home for lunch, or whatever.

And, so that was my job. It was paid, if I remember, slightly better than the paper round, but it had its bonuses because I used to come back to the bakery and Logie Birrell, at that time, he used to do what they called the 'hot plate' side, and that was always scones, pancakes and all this sort business on the big hotplate. And on a stove he had a big pot and he used to cook the doughnuts. So, of course, Ferguson's doughnuts had no hole in them. They didn't have the ring-type doughnut; he had a solid thing. They were very, very nice and I used to cook them, roll them

Some old shops - Aitken's sweetie shop (BHT collection), Robertson's boot and shoe shop (David R. Collin collection), and Crow the plumber's shop (BHT collection).

in the sugar, that was it. It was unfortunate, you tended to put your finger through a couple, you know, while you were doing it, but they had to be eaten then! But it was very nice, but that was what happened.

Then, of course, literally, John, my brother, [and] Logie, [went] off to the services and there was another chap, I forget his name, he went off, and this was the sort of thing that happened, suddenly, you know, little businesses, big businesses, men were whipped away, conscripted into the forces and I started, during that summer, staying on and helping, and I started doing scones, I made sponges, all this sort of thing, and learned quite a bit about baking. And, of course, I would work from, say, six in the morning, until about two to three o'clock in the afternoon. Then I went to the swimming pool, which was open, so it was a good summer. Things went on like that and I was reasonably happy, in a way, *but* looking for something else. And, of course, the place that really developed, or expanded very quickly, was Donibristle, the naval air repair yard. And I got in firstly, into the signals department, which was really just distributing all the signals coming in .....

Jim Harvey, retired joiner:

..... you've to bear in mind that a lot o' the work which we did, at one time, is now specialised wi' different contractors. For instance, people going on wi' new windows, new kitchens and central heating, of course, which was non-existent in my time, more or less. But that's another thing there's been a big advance on, is the central heating o' houses. I remember that the first lot o' central heating that was advertised, was in Kirkcaldy at one time. We had visitors; we went in there to see it. I was greatly taken with it, but they was houses with much smaller rooms than what I have here. And I asked Mr Black, the plumber, who was the contractor at that time, who modernised these houses, to come out. He didn't come any further than my front door. He says, "Oh, no," he says, "there's no use me coming any further. The size o' this, the type o' heating that we were introducing here," he says, "no use here, at all." So, in due course, the finer bore type o' central heating came into go, and well that was okay for here, and then an advance in heating boilers and things like that.

..... Well, at that time, there was about six of us in the town. My father started business actually when Mr Nimmo, Mr Henderson gave up business. Now Mr Henderson's workshop ..... at the bottom o' Cromwell Road, where there was a picture framing shop and something else ..... That was Mr Henderson's workshop. It took up quite an area. After that, it was a petrol station. And after that again, it's been several things.

Jim takes Hugh Fisher and Helen Mabon on a virtual tour of the west end of the High Street and Harbour Place, as they were in the old days.

..... There was another people took the grocer's shop after the Shanks had it. And then it was a butcher's shop at one time, and then it was a bookie's.

..... ye had McIntosh further down; they supplied the ships as well. But next to my entry, when I was young, was a fruit shop, and it was owned by the Archers, and they stayed across the road there, in a house, which has certainly been demolished. Duncan Williamson had a builder's yard there at one time. Next to that was this building where the Archers stayed, and down below it was a fishmonger.

..... And then there was a recess went back, and then there was houses there and a small shop there as well. Then further down, at the Green Tree, you had a saddler's shop, Wishart the Saddler, at that time. ..... And then that changed to be a hairdresser. And the man that had the hairdresser shop was a joiner to trade, and he worked in the shipyard.

..... And then, as you go down the street from here, there was, well, in the stone building you had Lawson, the ship agent, and then after that there was the pend where the workshop was. Next to that you had the entrance to a house, and then you had a small sweetie shop, which was a sweetie shop at the front and at the back was a barber's shop. That was McNiven's hairdressers shop. ..... Going further down from that, you had a small shop that more or less [sold] small fancy goods, and then you had Allan's chip shop. Going down from there, you had Jackson's ship chandlers, and Davidson's, the newsagents. Davidson's the newsagents changed hands several times, latterly to where Mr Gavin had his thing.

Then you had Well's Close, because there was a well in it at one time, and it was up that close that Jimmy Brooks had his workshop. The band hall was up there as well. Then you had a little confectioner's shop, which belonged to the Patersons. After that, you had McIntosh, the grocers, and after that you had Nisbet, which sold shoes and a' that sort o' thing. And then after that, you had a small baker's shop. No, before that you had Adamson, the hairdressers, and then this wee baker's shop.

..... As you go down Harbour Place, there was Anderson, the ironmonger, which, latterly, was Stephenson's ironmonger. Then you had Hanson, who dealt, more or less in clothing for the shipping side. After that, you had Jackson and Bruce, which were ship chandlers. Then you had the George Hotel. The George Hotel, at that time, had the Captains' Bar, the Officers' Bar, and the Crew's Bar. They were all kept separate.

After that you had a chip shop, before you came to Spice Row. When you went up Spice Row, which was an extension of Somerville Street, you had a workmen's home. After that, you had the Pacific Tavern ..... and then you had McKenzie's the grocers. .....

And after McKenzie, you went underneath the railway bridge and there was the Steamboat Tavern there, which was changed to the Pacific at one time and is now a house. Now that particular building was built when the railway came through. The railway built that property, because of what was there before. So they had to demolish one building and they built ..... the Steamboat Tavern and that.

Bill Stratton:

Well, we had all different fairs; five fairs, an Edinburgh Fair, they were quite good, like; I couldn't say that they were bad for business. It was always a wee bit extra, but I mean when Glasgow Fair, everybody was waiting for Glasgow Fair because when they came, by train, by buses, whatever it was, stayed for a fortnight solid. So every shopkeeper had benefit, whatever it was. They came with twenty, thirty pounds, in those days that was a lot of money, you know. And they said, "Well, I brought it, get something for my missus, something for my daughter, something for my son." ..... Put ten pounds on the counter, he says, "Get them something each." You know, that's how it was, no hanky-panky, ... money just. And then of course, I was across the road from the Ex-Servicemen's Club, that was 'bla, bla, bla' till midnight .....

..... We had tins, Coca-Cola we eventually got there, direct bottles and the rest. ..... in the beginning [it was just] the Coca-Cola, no' like just now. But Plummer was the main supplier, there was cases and cases of lemonade sold, and the empty bottles coming back, kids collecting them on the Links. I don't know, five pence, I think a bottle or something, I think I had to give them; quite happy spending it again for sweets and everything! So I was all business, exchange. ..... We were practically double supply the week for the Games Day.

You know, was the rock, at least, and then fancy goods; we had china from Liverpool, we had china, in fact I've a cup here. This was our best seller with still my name below - William Stratton, 122 High Street, Burntisland. Aye, and that was a seller. That was about fifty pence, I think it was, or whatever it was. It was a cup and [there was] a thistle one as well, and then we had the armchair television set with a wee plate and a cup on it, like, and oh, there was spoons, oh yes, different silver spoons, Burntisland. All the souvenirs, that was during the summer time it was going!

..... at one time, when a bus came in the morning, by the end of the day they just went back, you know, seven, eight, nine o'clock, well, those people from Glasgow, they stayed a fortnight for holiday. They had accommodation in the town, or hotels, different things, like. Some came just for the weekend, you know, depends how they felt about it, but they came, mostly the full day. Was a full day spent in Burntisland, there was no just coming in and out.

..... a wholesaler came to me and says, "Mr Stratton, you have more stock than I have." I says, "How is that?" He says, "Oh, you're having direct, I have direct too, but seemingly you're selling more than I do." The wholesaler from Kirkcaldy, he came to my shop. So we sold, really, a lot, a lot. I mean, I went two, three times, oh, more than that, every month, practically, you know, from Terry's, from Duncan's, from Mackintosh's, all the chocolates, you know, novelties and whatever it was, fancy goods for Christmas, Santa Clauses and different things,

Betty Traynor:

I left school at fourteen years old and went to work in Cowan's Restaurant on the High Street at the bottom of Black's Close, near the police station. My job in the forenoon from eight to eleven was to do all the cleaning and scrubbing to get ready for the doors to open before lunchtime. I went home at eleven o'clock to get changed into my waitress outfit and went back to work to serve the customers and later on wash up the dishes. Quite often if we were busy we had to work till six or seven at night. We were really busy during the summer months with visitors to the town and with the 'Willie Muir' ferry boat running from Granton to Burntisland, this also gave us lots of customers.

Cathie Watson:

Oh definitely, oh yes, [my mother did all her shopping in Burntisland]. ..... there was Gray the draper, Duncanson the draper, and Thomson the grocer. Oh, [she shopped every day] practically and we got milk at the door of course. The milkman arrived every morning. So that came and sometimes they kept butter and eggs. You could get them from the milkman too but apart from that everything else had to be brought or carried. Oh yes, she used to shop every afternoon practically.

Oh no, no fridge. You had to get milk, the horse brought the milk.

Oh now, Leitch, we got our beef from Leitch. Now who else? There was another one on the other side. That would be Brown. ..... We had meat every day. Now I never touch it. But oh yes, you had to have your mince and tatties and soup, every day. And I couldn't bear soup when I was a girl. Now I love it. And they're all home made of course but mother grew a lot in the garden, brussels sprouts and cabbage, lettuce, leeks. We grew all these things ourselves and we had gooseberry bushes. We had strawberries. We had blackcurrants and oh we had a lovely summer-house in the back garden at Oakdene. I remember it was a lovely place. What else did we have? Apple trees, five apple trees we had, two standards.

Cherry Rigby:

I left school when I was fifteen, went to work in Willie Barclay's, the decorator, where I served in the shop and I did his books. There was Willie Jackson, 'Pansy' Shand, Bert White and Stan Robertson were the painters. ..... I was taught books by Mr Painter ..... he was the teacher at the night school.

..... [at that time the shops were] freezing cold! There was no heating at all, in that shop, summer or winter. It was freezing. Mark you, there was plenty shops. There was a lot o' shops. Right from the bottom of the High Street right up. [And] there was up the Kirkgate, up the Kirkgate, yes. There was Bisset's, the sweetie shop, and McIntosh.

..... Willie Barclay's shop was at the side o' Martin, the joiner, at the pend on the High Street, on the south side o' the High Street, the cold side o' the High Street. It was freezing that side. ..... Jim Turner was in [that] shop. That's where Willie Barclay's shop was. [Andrew Young had his studio] right across from there. ..... wasn't he up the Pend from Fairlie, the painter? That was before Ferguson. .....

Willie 'Wan Paw'. 'Wan Paw'. One hand, paw. Yes, he used to come wi' the milk, and wi' the pitcher. And he delivered our milk. Willie 'Wan Paw'. ..... I think he worked for Bert Grant. ..... From the Grange.

Jimmy Wilson:

My first job was a message boy wi' John Graham the butcher, and I was there, served my time right up through till 1936, when I went to ask him for an increase in my wages. From 1929 until the time I asked him for the rise, I was getting, in old money, 22 shillings a week, one pound two shillings. ..... I asked him for a rise because I was working from seven o'clock in the morning, till seven, eight, nine o'clock at night, ten o'clock sometimes. Christmas time and New Year time it was ten o'clock, eleven o'clock, plucking chickens and whatever.

..... we worked in the shop. And I also, I never wanted to be a butcher who worked in a shop. What I wanted to be was a slaughterman, because we went, we did all our own killin' across in the old slaughterhouse, across there. Across at the Lammerlaws. That building at the Lammerlaws when you go just across the bridge, you turn right and there's a building away down in the bottom. That building was opposite the Dive Bunker.

[How many butchers?] - there was John Graham, Peter Garrick, Bob Brown, that's three, Eddie Danks was four, the Co-operative was five .....

..... I wanted to be a slaughterman, but there wasnae any vacancies for slaughtermen at that [time], and anyway I would have had to, if I'd wanted to be, or got a job, I'd have had to travel to even Kirkcaldy or Edinburgh or Glasgow and that was out of the question.

But that, I mean, serving the public in a shop, is the worst job in the world. You always get somebody moaning and groaning about something.

I went and asked [Graham] for a pay rise, and he offered me two shillings, so that was gonna take me up to 24 shillings a week, after being there from 1929 to 1936. And he said he had no money, ... times were hard, but he was the only man who had a car standing outside his door. And I told him what to do with his two shillings, and I went home and said to my mother that one of my customers knew that I wasnae very happy with my work and [had] said that, when the time came, that I was leaving, or packing up, if I let her know, she would speak to her husband and I would get a job in the shipyard.

..... so I went home to my mother and I said that I was packing up, and she says, "Yer daft." I says, "Why?" She says, "It's coming up for Xmas time, you'll lose a' yer Xmas tips." I said, "Oh, I never thought o' that." So I hung on till after Xmas, then when, after Xmas, and I got, well at that time you would maybe pick up, what, seven, eight quid, you know, in Xmas tips. That was a lot of money, in these days. ..... and then I went in one day and I told him I was packing it up and I went down the shipyard.

Albert Gunn:

..... But if you got your lemonade bottles, jam jars were the favourite, and return them, then you got your penny. And there used to be a little sweet shop at the foot of the Kirkgate, Bisset's, and next door to that was, right on the corner, it became Möller's, I can't remember the name it was before Möller's, but it was a grocer's shop, and then on the opposite corner, which has now been demolished, was Stocks's, and that was sweets and that, and that was two sisters ran that. And, strangely enough, when the picture house closed, they actually moved to the shop next door to the new picture house at the Porte and they had the sweet shop there, until they retired, in fact they lived in the flat above there.

Violet McFarlane:

Well I worked in a tobacconist and confectioners in Rose Street or was it Thistle Street? Rose Street! It was Miss Hutton who had the shop, the same Miss Hutton who held the kinderspiels, she gave me a nice reference when I left. Then, when I left there, my last job was Ferguson the Baker in the High Street, just across from the bottom of Lothian Street. Then I left there in 1938 to come to Renton to be married. My late husband came from Renton and I have lived here ever since and loved it although I still have a soft spot for Burntisland.

The Laundry

Annie Christie:

I left the school at fourteen; left on the Friday and started work on the Monday. I was in the laundry office for a week, just, and then another girl got the job, so the manageress, she was a friend o' one o' our neighbours and she asked me if I'd like to work inside the laundry and I said, "Oh, aye." I was dying to work, you know. So I worked in the laundry for a good few years, in fact there was quite a few of us from Meadowfield worked in the laundry. We just had to go down the road and over the field and into the laundry.

..... they had a big roller thing, you know, it was red hot, and they put sheets and tablecloths and that through, they were really wet, but they put them through and you had to hold them till they were dry and then they were folded up. Then there was ironers; there was a row of ironers, you know, wi' ironing tables, and then there was the packing at the top where, after all the clothes were washed and dried, they had numbers on them, and there was racks. You had to put each article in the rack by the numbers, and then once you got them finished, towels, sheets or whatever it was, you had to check them with a list that you got and then you had to put them a', you had to wrap them up in paper and put their labels on them for the van man to take away. So I quite liked it, ... it was hot in the laundry, mind you.

..... [It served] Aberdour, Inverkeithing, Rosyth and Donibristle; Burntisland, of course.

There would be maybe about fifteen or sixteen [working there], I think. 'Cause there was a man, he worked the machines, you know, it was like big things that they put the washing in and they went round and round. And then there was, like, what we call spin dryers, but they were called 'hydros', put the washing in, big iron things and it drained the water out them.

THE BURNTISLAND
STEAM & HAND
LAUNDRY

Is located in an open situation, at DICK TERRACE, away from dust or smoke nuisance.

The Buildings are airy and well lighted, and are fitted up with the best appliances. Our Workers have been carefully selected and are under the direct supervision of a thoroughly capable and expert Manageress.

All Orders receive prompt attention, and goods are returned Clean and Fresh, with UTMOST DISPATCH.

ʬ

Goods received from Shipping are washed separately and returned to Vessels on Shortest Notice.

ʬ

Consult our Price List and you will find that the prices stated compare very favourably with any other good Laundry, while we guarantee good work.

General Interior View of Burntisland Laundry. (*Now under New Management*)

It is a fallacy to think that articles of clothing washed in

Rotary
Washing Machines

of the most recent construction (such as ours are) are subjected to more wear and tear than by the old laborious Hand Washing, proof of which will be demonstrated to you, if you favour us with a visit to our works.

In order, however, to meet the requirements of all our Customers, we will, if so desired, wash by hand articles specially mentioned.

ʬ

A personal call or letter to the New Manageress (Miss M'Cartney) will receive
PROMPT ATTENTION.

ʬ

Special Terms for Large Quantities, Hotels, Boarding Houses, etc., on application.

Section of Washing Department, Burntisland Laundry.

*A comprehensive advertisement for the Burntisland Steam and Hand Laundry.
BHT collection.*

Chapter 3

The Second World War

PETER ANDERSON
ROBERT A. BEST
JAMES C. BIRRELL
LOGIE BIRRELL
KEITH BOUFFLER
PHILIP J. CARNIE
J. L. C. CUNNINGHAM
WILLIAM DRYSDALE
JOHN B. FERGUSON
JOHN FOTHERINGHAM
DUNCAN FRASER
JAMES L. GILMOUR
ALFRED GRAY
W. DUNCAN HARROW

ARTHUR IRONS
WILLIAM E. LYLE
JOHN McCOW
WILLIAM McKELVIE
A. M. McLAUCHLAN
HENRY MOYES
CHARLES MOYNES
HENRY E. MUIR
WILLIAM NAIRN
JOHN P. PATERSON
JAMES REID
THOMAS A. ROBERTSON
JAMES RONALDSON
HAMISH ROSS

ROBERT B. RUSSELL
GEORGE C. SAUNDERS
JOHN SCOBIE
ROBERT R. SCOTLAND
ANDREW C. R. SHAND
DAVID SIMPSON
H. E. SIMPSON
WILLIAM SMITH
JAMES S. THOMPSON
WILLIAM TURNBULL
JOSEPH VALENTINE
JOHN WILKIE
JOHN WILKIE
JOHN S. WILSON

Above - the Second World War panel on Burntisland War Memorial.

This book is being published in the same year as the sixtieth anniversary of the end of the Second World War. It is therefore fitting that we are able to reproduce here extracts from recorded reminiscences which related to the war. These include four personal stories from individuals who live in Burntisland, but whose backgrounds and wartime experiences are very different.

Air Raids

Walter Carstairs:

[Greenmount House] was beautiful, because, I remember, during the war, we were stationed there, because it was so high up and you could get a lovely view o'er. And I was in charge of this, I was a leading fireman, at that time, and that's where we were appointed that night of Clydebank, the big Clydebank. Oh, terrible bombing. Now we went up to the top of the house and we could see the planes coming up the Forth, one after the other, German planes that bombed Clydebank.

Annie Christie:

..... that was when the bombs were dropped. My mother and I, we were washing the tea dishes when we heard this plane, it was very, very low, so I said to mother, "That plane's low. I'm going out to see," and it was just sort o' skiffing the rooftops, you know? And of course, the next thing I just heard this bang, and everything sort o' shuddered. So we never thought any more about it. We didna' know it was a German plane, of course. So the next day we were all up looking at the thing 'cause it was just up from the wee cottages. And this man had been walking his dog and he heard this ticking sound in the hole. So he must have reported it, 'cause when we came up from our work on the teatime, we were stopped at the Toll by the police, told to go to the Erskine Church, that we were not to go up the road, we couldn't get into our houses. So we didnae stay in the Erskine Church at night, of course, because my mother ..... was friendly with a policeman's wife and we went to their house in Links Place, but everybody else had to sleep in the Erskine Church hall for the night till the bomb was disconnected, like, and then we got back the next day. But we were here when the bombs were dropped. .....

Well, you never know when they might have gone off, that's right. But there was a squad o' soldiers came and they were disconnecting the bomb. We called them the suicide squad. But there was a land mine dropped at the back of it, away over the hill. It was like a quarry, it was some size, but we were in our shelters that night, 'cause it was the night of the Clydebank Blitz, and we were in the shelter the whole night. [The shelters were] at the bottom o' the garden there. [An Anderson shelter[1],] just an earth floor and sometimes they were wet and sometimes they wernae. Sat in there and never thought anything about it, mind. [My family and] the lady across the road from us, she had about five wee ones, they were a' wee, just one after the other. And her husband would never get out his bed at night to go to the shelter, so my mother and I had to go across and help out wi' a' the wee ones. But Chrissie wouldnae go into our shelter because she said it was too much. She used to go to the one up next door. She wouldnae go in it at a'. But they felt sorry for the woman as well, because she was worried about her children, you know. They were a' just wee tots. But we sat there the whole night. We just sat and I remember my father was always standing outside watching the flares and that, you know. And I says, "Oh, listen to that!" He says, "Ah well, it's a' right as long as you can hear it." ..... we just got up and went away to our work the next day, we never thought anything about it. Nope.

Janet Agnew and Sadie Edwards;

Sadie Edwards: I was nine when [the war] broke out, and as I said about the air raid shelters, I can remember walking up, or being led up to the Castle and sitting until the 'all clear'. Actually *in* the kitchen area. They had a main door where the owners of the Castle [went in], it was privately owned at that time. And then along the building, there was a little door where the servants, and we went in there, along the corridor and sat in the kitchen.

[The servants' quarters were] our air raid shelter, and we had to stay in there because of the thickness of the walls ..... it was to be safe, if we were ever bombed. Then we were all supplied with air raid shelters, the Anderson, corrugated iron. Every household had one, and you had to take it in the garden. .....

---

[1] A corrugated iron shelter supplied by the Government free of charge (unless you earned over £250 a year, when it cost £7). It was largely submerged in a four feet deep hole which had to be dug for it.

Janet Agnew: Two families in ours. We had to go up and mother would take us up in the middle of the night and, of course, the first thing that went was the deed box. That was always taken, every night we went up there, but we used to go up religiously. [The deed box] was where all the insurance policies and everything were kept. I've still got it.

Sadie Edwards: We had a suitcase, my mother put her's in a suitcase; insurance policies, birth, you know.

Janet Agnew: Birth certificates, all the certificates.

Sadie Edwards: That went to the air raid [shelters.] We shared with a family as well, because, well, my father was dead, we didn't have anybody to dig our shelter; it was partly done, but it wasn't inhabitable, so we shared with the Beavers, and they had bunk beds in it. And blankets. And I can remember being *taken*, because when I went to sleep, I went to sleep. They used to dress me, walk me there and waken me up to get home. And sometimes they would say they'd been in the shelter during the night and I didn't know, but they had taken me, they'd dressed me and taken me and brought me back, and I'd slept through it all!

Janet Agnew: ..... I would waken up because as I said the siren was next door to us, on top of the picture house and, no, I used to walk up. But latterly, further on in the war, I joined the Girls Training Corps ..... if the ARP was out, if you had messages to take somewhere, you took messages and that was about it. But it was fun.

Janet Agnew: ..... actually, the schoolhouse had incendiary bombs dropped on it, janitor's house.

Sadie Edwards: Mr Hendry lived in it then. Then they dropped the bombs on the Binn.

Janet Agnew: One was a time bomb, which they set off during school hours. Things were falling off the ceiling. We thought it was great!

Betty Traynor:

During the war we lived in a house at the corner of Black's Close and the Spice, as we called it, up the hill from the sailors' home. That's at the far end of Somerville Street towards the harbour area. We lived in a block of six which included old Mrs Motion, Mrs Lindsay, the Lawson family, the Robsons and the Lairds, on the bottom floor. With the war on, there was a great community spirit and we were all very happy and even with the shortages of things we all managed to help each other out if we could.

When the air raid siren blew, even in the middle of the night, we had to get out the house and run about 50 yards along Somerville

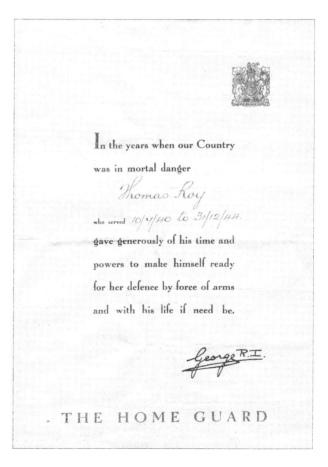

In the years when our Country

was in mortal danger

Thomas Roy

who served 10/7/40 to 31/12/44.

gave generously of his time and

powers to make himself ready

for her defence by force of arms

and with his life if need be.

George R.I.

. THE HOME GUARD

Janet Agnew's father, Thomas Roy, was in the Home Guard. This is the certificate he received in recognition of his service.

Street to an old converted basement of an empty derelict house taken over by the ARP. It was very difficult for Joe and me as we had four wee girls to cope with, and when we got to the shelter, as it was usually damp and far too overcrowded. When I think of it now it could not possibly take in all the families round about, if they all turned up. Sometimes we had a good time in the shelter with a sing-song and a good blether.

As time went on you began to think that the air raids was beginning to slow down and it was as well to take a chance and leave the girls sleeping in their own bed. As I say, it was not easy getting four, and later five little girls out of bed to run along the street, and so later on in the war we decided to stay at home when the siren blew.

One day, a group of the women in the Guild were up at the priest's house up on Leven Street. We were in the church hall which was beneath the house. We were preparing for a social evening that was to be held in the hall that night. When the siren blew, and we heard the planes, all the women ran out into the garden and we could see all the German bombers flying up the Forth. We found out later that this was them going to blitz Clydebank.

During the war we had to be very careful and not show any light out of the doors and windows so we had to have blackout curtains. The ARP wardens came round the streets checking every night and you'd be in trouble if you forgot. The other big problem was if you had to go out at night as it was pitch black sometimes and all you had was your wee torch shining down on the pavement. I remember quite often going up to see my mum and dad at Leven Street and you were in danger of banging into or falling over something, so you had to be very careful.

Albert Gunn:

..... I also got involved in the local, what they called the AFS, the Auxiliary Fire Service, and they had a trailer pump at Burntisland, and Davie Martin that I mentioned who is a local joiner ..... he was the leading fireman, I think [that] was his title. And the rest of the men were local tradesmen. I can remember Davie, was it Davie[2] Reekie, there was a plumber and people like that. Martin had a sort of flat-back little truck and that, of course, towed the trailer.

..... as soon as the air raid siren went, we had to report. And that's when it got a bit messy, because, you know you got tucked up in bed on a winter's night and all warm and the air raid siren would go off about two in the morning or something. And my mother, of course, never missed it. That was '40, '41, '42.

We had two, well only one *real* incident in Burntisland, and that was, I was in the swimming pool, literally, going up and down. It was the fifty yard pool about seven o'clock in the evening, summer time, and I heard this aircraft and looked up and here was a Heinkel 111 coming over from Edinburgh direction and flying off over the Binn And I'm swimming away, and suddenly his bomb doors opened and down they came, and it was incendiaries that dropped. So I thought, "Oh, crikey!" No air raid siren, of course, no warning or anything had gone, which was typical. And so, of course, I dashed and got dried, dressed and went dashing off and the bombs landed on what is now Toll Park, except for one and that went through the roof of the janitor's house, the school janitor's house, in Ferguson Place. And we had all had instruction: incendiary bombs, you put sand on them, not water. So, of course, being pretty good, intelligent chaps they got into the roof, took a hose up and turned the hose on and they did more damage with the water - they brought the ceiling down, I think, trying to put this thing out - than ever the bomb would have done. And that was the air raid on Burntisland. .....

I think that was the same aircraft that had some high explosive bombs on it. It dropped them in Leith, and hit a distillery warehouse. Well, they reckon they were scooping whisky out the gutter! It was running down the gutters .....

---

[2] Probably Andrew Reekie.

The other one was the raid, I'm sure it was '42, when I was going out, a November evening I think, and I heard this aircraft, and again, as I say, working at Donibristle, you knew all the engines. ..... And this was a German, and he flew up, very dark night, and he flew right up, shall we say, parallel with the river, Kinghorn, over the Binn, roughly, and headed on up towards Aberdour, but during the war you had search lights on Inchcolm and Inchmickery, you'd searchlights at Kinghorn and Inchkeith sweeping the approach, up the river, and obviously looking for submarines probably, or any other ship coming up. And it was almost a perfect marker, 'cause this chap went up, and I could hear him go round, turning, and he probably turned about the Forth Bridge, roughly, and came round and then he came in.

Now it was a dark, very dark night, and I was going down, there was a youth club in the Church Hall at that time, and I was going down for about half past seven and, anyway, I stood in the back garden at Shepherd Crescent and I saw him go over. I could see a light in the nose, which was probably the bomb-aimer, and he was very low. I could see the outline, more or less, of the plane; I couldn't recognize what it was. And I thought, crikey, he'll be lucky to clear the Binn. And he flew, he came in over the river, over the shipyard and the aluminium works, of course, over the Binn and was gone. Now I didn't hear a sound, and he dropped, I think it was, four bombs and they all hit the base of the Binn, just opposite the houses at Meadowfield, you know the newer ones as you're going up the Cowdenbeath Road? Well, on that field there.

Without a doubt [his target was the docks and the aluminium] and he wasn't far out. When you think of it, it's not a big distance and of course the great excitement was, three of the bombs had exploded in, just in the earth, in the field, but one didn't, and, of course, then an unexploded bomb, and everyone was warned the next day. I don't know if they used too much explosives to blow it up or what they did, but it smashed a few windows in the Kirkton area. That was the war in Burntisland.

Other Wartime Memories

Annie Christie:

..... Aye, it was busy. There was a lot o' the forces, a lot o' Polish soldiers here, they were stationed at Dunearn. And then there was soldiers stationed at Ged's Mill [and] the Palais, and you used to get a lot o' the sailors from Rosyth came to the Palais as well. Oh it was busy.

Albert Gunn:

..... one of my elder brothers, John, he's walking along the side of the pool, the west side of the pool with a chap called Logie Birrell and they were carrying a basket because they were both apprentices with Ferguson the baker, serving their time. And Logie and John, immediately war started, ... they were both away literally within weeks of war being declared, and John went in the army, Logie went in the navy, and Logie lost his life in the Atlantic, the ship was torpedoed during the war.

Norman Mackie:

A few months ago I was thinking about things that happened in the past, when I was called up, standing on the platform in November 1941, the only soul on the platform, with a paper parcel to send my clothes back. I was bound for Bedford and Cardington. Cardington was the base of the RAF where I was going to join up. That as a lad is a lasting memory, also with my RAF number which I can still repeat to anybody.

Then it came back to me, in 1938 when the country was preparing for war and I was in the British Aluminium Company and we had an architects' department, and one of the architects he travelled from Edinburgh each day. He was away with the Territorial Army in Scotland camping and he had informed his friends in the architects' department that they would be coming to Burntisland on the Friday of this particular month in 1938. He was a member of the London Scottish Territorials. So when we got word, the boys all went to the Toll to see the London Scottish march down. We saw them passing the distillery down the Cowdenbeath Road and the assembly must have been about 200 territorials all in their kilts, the sand coloured the London Scottish wore. They stopped at the Binn Lodge and assembled into order and all the various vehicles were behind, and the pipe band, they struck up, and they marched from the Binn Lodge, right to the Toll, down Cromwell Road, turned left and went out to Greenmount Farm, where they camped; and broke camp the next day and joined the ferry at Burntisland across to Edinburgh, where they were going to embark on trains back down to London. Now that was the most wonderful sight to see ..... these young men, and we saw this young man marching down, never saw him again. He was killed in Singapore. The London Scottish.

..... It was a sight I'll never forget, and I was just saying to myself, I wonder if anyone else in Burntisland remembers that sight. The London Scottish marching through Burntisland.

..... So many memories of my rugby friends who died ..... one who carried the legs to Douglas Bader who had aluminium legs. ..... a Burntisland fellow [was one of the crew] that flew them out to replace them when [Bader] was captured ..... I played rugby with Lawrence Lawson. 'LL' we used to call him. His father was [a Public Assistance official] and Lawrence joined up and became a [Sergeant in the RAF, in a squadron that flew Blenheims.] ..... when Douglas Bader was shot down he had artificial legs and they were dented or broken, so he had to have them replaced. They made arrangements with the Germans who had captured him to send replacements, to replace the ..... aluminium legs. ..... [Lawrence was one of the crew that flew on the mercy mission] and dropped them over where [Bader] was a prisoner of war. [Although promised a safe passage the plane came under fire.[3]] ..... I was friendly with Lawrence and his sister Margaret was a great friend of Cathie Watson and the last time we were at a funeral at the Erskine Church, Cathie Watson and Daphne and I, and who was there but Margaret Lawson.

Betty Traynor:

Food was pretty scarce during the war but of course we had ration books, you see, we had coupons for most things we wanted, clothes, food, sweets etc, although the shops didn't always have what you needed but you would generally get what you were entitled to.

There were Polish soldiers billeted in houses and halls all over the town with the Palais de Danse as the main barracks. There were soldiers guarding the dock area and the Lammerlaws. I remember huge concrete blocks all along the promenade and wooden poles all over the sand bank right out to the Black Rock and Pettycur. The shipyard and aluminium works had voluntary Home Guard on duty outside working hours and many of the men in the town joined up and my husband Joe was one of them. Later on my brother Dan joined the Parachute Regiment and Alan was in the Royal Artillery Territorial Army.

The shipyard was very busy during the war time especially. There must have been at least two thousand men and women working there. I remember most clearly the perpetual noise of the riveters and caulkers banging away all day long. We had to warn the girls constantly not to go near the High Street at tea time as there must have been twenty or more double decker buses racing up the street taking the workers home to Kirkcaldy, Cowdenbeath and Dunfermline.

---

[3] Although Lawrence survived that mission, sadly he was killed later in 1941. He is buried in Tripoli, North Africa.

Jim Harvey:

..... after the war was declared, I got twelve months postponement from call-up, and after that time I had to go into Government work, which was the shipyard. But before I went into the shipyard, I got a circular from the Government asking me if I was prepared to change my trade to a fitter. And this I was prepared to do, and in due course, I had to go through a training course in Glasgow; at the railway works in Glasgow. After that period of time, I was posted through to Donibristle, which was the main RAF repair yard, and I was there for the duration of the war. After that. I was made a WT charge hand, eventually, and it was there that I met my wife.

Cherry Rigby:

[At] the beginning of 1940, ... I took the King's Shilling, and went into the forces, and I only got my father's signature, for the simple reason he thought he could claim me beside him at Kinghorn! And then to his horror, I wasn't, that didn't work. He wanted me to be posted so he could keep an eye on me in Kinghorn.

..... King's Own Scottish Borderers. Yep, Berwick-on-Tweed. That was where I

In 1943, Isa Duncanson and her friends went guising with the aim of raising some money for the Army's overseas Cigarette Fund. They collected thirty-eight shillings and Isa sent it off. She received this thank you letter, personally signed by Monty (General, later Field Marshall, Bernard Montgomery).
Isa Duncanson collection.

worked, where I was sent. I didn't know they existed. To me, there was only one regiment, of course; there was the artillery, that was it.

..... my Mother was called up to munitions. In Kinghorn. There was a place in Kinghorn, fortunately. They were doing, it's something to do with Admiralty. I don't know what ..... it was at the back of where the Town Hall is.

I was in the Dental Corps. I wasn't in the Dental Corps when I first went, I was in the Quartermaster's, but then I went into the Dental Corps. ..... I was posted to Berwick-on-Tweed and then ..... we were with an ITC, and then we were ..... en masse taken up to Inverness and posted there where we were loathed, because we had put the Camerons out the barracks, and they didn't like us in Inverness. We were there twelve months, posted back to Edinburgh and that was the worst time in my ..... whole military career! I didn't like, it was too near home! That was my trouble. I was too near home.

..... if I was away, posted away, it never entered my head, I wasn't homesick in the least, but taken to Edinburgh, oh, out to Colinton, I hated it there, hated it. ..... that was when I left the Quartermaster's and went into the Dental Corps. Was posted to Freshfield, near Formby in Liverpool, and I loved that. Then I was posted, from there, I was into Aldershot and I was in Aldershot just about Dieppe time. And the Canadians ....., when they came back from Dieppe, they went berserk ..... They were so angry about it, because it was such a shambles. It was so unnecessary. The death was totally unnecessary. ..... it was totally bad planning; it really was ..... it was a terrible time.

..... I met my husband in Berwick-on-Tweed. ..... he was a Mancunian, who was in the Green Howards. We met on the border, did oor coortin' on the border, and then he was posted to India, and we never seen each other for about three years, never. And then he came home. ..... I stayed in till 1946, and then I got, took my demob then. Got married, went to stay in Manchester and couldn't settle there. I'm not a city person, in any shape or form, and I did like to see the sea. I did like to see the sea where I was. And I came back here in 1950. So that was ten years I was away.

Albert Gunn's Story

I can remember, I was eighteen, I thought, I'll go in, and M and M's became the recruiting office for the RAF, and I came out the pictures one night and I just walked in, and filled in a form and that was that. ..... my mother and father didn't say much, but their attitude was that they weren't very much in favour of what I was doing.

..... I had this interview, and in the end they said, "Well, yes, we're going to accept you," for what they called PNB training, that was Pilot, Navigator or Bombing.

..... I said, "Oh well, I'll go as an air gunner then." So that was in, I think November of '42 and I got a letter calling me up, I had to report to Lord's cricket ground in London on the 15th March 1943. And that was me in the RAF.

..... we had a brief time at Bridgnorth in Shropshire, then up to Dalcross, which is now Inverness Airport, and that's where we started flying ..... you were literally  eating, sleeping, flying, you know. Summertime, the weather was good, so we did the course and both Bobby Russell and I were still more or less together ..... and we both came on leave in July of '43; and shows on the Links, everything just as normal, carrying on. We were then qualified, supposed to be, as Sergeant Air Gunners.

Albert continues his story, moving forward to December 1943.

..... I think that night, the idea was that there was over 800 aircraft bombing Berlin that night, and it was in three waves. Well a wave, you maybe had ten minutes, so you had about 800 aircraft bombing in under half an hour. So as you can appreciate, if everybody was on course and at the right timing, you had an awful lot of aircraft very close together. And this was one of the big dangers, collision with your own aircraft. However, we'd no problems at all and it was heavy cloud. We'd climbed cloud quite a bit; in fact, we were over the Dutch coast, over Holland, before we actually got to the top of the cloud.

..... Anyhow, we pressed on, we got above the cloud and everything was going according to plan. The weather was clear then, apart from, you know, cloud underneath, and I can remember we could see Hanover, the defences there; somebody had been off course and had been shot at ..... our starboard outer engine started to act up, and the engineer could do nothing with it, and he just said it was losing power, and he said the fuel seemed all right. We had plenty fuel, ... but in the end, we had to feather, shut the engine down, feather the prop and we carried on, which was the best way, because to turn round in the middle of about 700 to 800 aircraft was a dangerous business, because everyone was at different heights.

..... we carried on and we were maintaining height, when the starboard inner started to do the same thing. Again the engineer tried his best to check everything, check the fuel and all the rest of it and no problems, and we had to cut the inner engine ..... It was awkward for the pilot. So anyhow, we then had a discussion, we said, "Well, look, there is no point now," we were losing height. "All we can do is turn back." So we jettisoned the bomb load, which really made little difference, because we were only on the two engines, but we turned, were heading back and we had thoughts of *getting* back. Then it was, well, maybe we'll make the North Sea, which I didn't fancy at all, and then, possibly, we would make Holland. So, anyway, the next thing was, the port inner started to do the same thing. And, in the end, Andy the pilot, said, "Look," he said, "I don't think we're going to get much further, be prepared to bail out." So, the inner, eventually, was actually shut down and we were flying on one engine, which was going full bore. It was the port outer that was going, but anyway, I got out. I was in the mid upper turret, and we used to carry two pigeons with us, which I always thought was a daft idea. The idea being, if you came down in the sea, you could send a message back by pigeon with your position.

..... all we knew was, we were over Europe somewhere! ..... as you can appreciate at sea, unless you have a very, very good pinpoint where someone is, you've a job to find them, particularly a dinghy. Anyway, we were struggling on and I used my parachute to hold the two pigeons, the two boxes, in position. So I got out the turret. Now, we'd never, any of us, put a parachute on.

..... you'd to remember you pull the handle, that was the main thing. So what I did was, in the Halifax, the centre section of the wing comes right through. I mean, obviously, you've got a huge centre section, which goes out either side of the fuselage, and then the rest of the wing is added on. And I thought, well, I had to climb over the centre section, which is awkward, then I had to go along, go past the pilot and then go down into the nose, below, underneath the instrument panel, and then there was the hole in the floor to jump out. So, I thought the best way to do it, is I'll clip my 'chute on and off we go. So I clipped the 'chute on, to find to my horror, it pulled the hook, the main pack out, pulled the strings, broke the strings on my shoulder and the parachute and all the harness landed at my feet.

So, I sort of folded it on top and then held it, so I then [was] faced with getting over the centre section, one-handed, if you like, holding the 'chute, which I did, and I was determined, and it was funny how, I suppose you would say silly, not silly things, but things go through your mind. I thought I must remember which side the handle's on, because if I let go of the 'chute when I got out, if this thing floated away from me, I would have been going down without the 'chute being opened. Anyway, I can remember going past Andy the pilot, and there was only Andy at the controls and our wireless operator left, the others had gone, and I got down to the nose and there's a hatch, which seems far too small to get out, but my idea was, people used to say, "..... Make sure you give a good shove, because there's a tail wheel that might catch you," just to cheer you up. And I thought, well, I'm never going to be able to push myself much, one-handed, as it were. So anyway, I thought I mustn't waste time, because when I got past the cockpit, we were not much over 2,000 feet by that time.

We were getting down, and there was still two of them going to be after me, and I could see Andy ..... those two engines were just going to roll you over. Anyhow, got to this hole, which was pitch black. We were in ten-tenth cloud, it was actually pouring buckets of rain and all you got was this, like, mist coming up, and that's where you had to go out. So, out I went, and I just had an impression of the aircraft going past, and I pulled the handle, and, fortunately, it did open with quite a jerk and I had a bit of a stiff neck for a few days afterwards ..... there I was, happily in my 'chute, in cloud, in rain and then I heard the aircraft turning and I thought, oh crikey, it's coming back, but it wasn't, it was going over and going down.

..... I was quite, I suppose you would say, calm about the whole thing, and, as I say, the aircraft exploded, hit the ground obviously with a tremendous bang because we still had a lot of fuel on board which went up ..... I started then to swing, and somebody, I think somewhere somebody said, "Well if you swing one way, you pull on your straps the other," and I was still trying to work this out when I realised there was a darker bit just to my right and, the thing was, I was swinging back and I hit the ground and that was it! I went through some wee bushy trees, or something, but I was on the edge of a field, and there was a road within 20 feet of where I landed .....

Not a clue [where I was], and I took off my harness, took off my 'Mae West' jacket thing, which I didn't need, helmet obviously, and got the 'chute, wrapped it all up and, we were told, usually, get rid of your gear and get away from where the aircraft's come down, if you are reasonably close to it. So I thought, well, I'm not all that far, wherever I was, so anyway, as I say, it was raining quite steadily; not a breath of wind and I was just getting that done when a car came along. That's how I found out I was near a road, this car came along. So I hid down in these bushes and the car went past, and so I thought, right, I knew the aircraft was to my left, I thought. There was still the glow in the sky where it was burning. So I thought, well I'll go right, and off I went, and of course, I heard music then and I was walking into a village and there was a local dance going on and you could hear, obviously, just a typical wee village hall like you would see in any wee town.

..... I came up past this dance hall, and I thought, I've got to keep going through the village now. And as I approached, the road branched like a 'Y', and right on the junction of the 'Y' was a soldier and a girl having a good snog! You know, I could see them and, obviously, there was no lights, really, but I could see them. So I thought, crikey, so anyway, I went to the right, and off I went. And I walked a long way, I reckoned I walked for four hours anyway, if not more, and I was getting tired, I was getting wet and we were told, "Get away from where the aircraft came down. Find somewhere to hide up for the night and then assess your situation in daylight." So I thought, right, pitch black, out in the country. You can imagine it was a dark night, cloud right down almost to the ground and, you know, raining and miserable night. So, each time I could see, like a farm building, or that, went to approach, dogs started barking, so I kept going. And finally, I was going up this country road and I heard someone behind me. I thought, oh crikey, who could this be? And I actually spoke up a bit and said, "Who's there?" or, "Is that you, Gerry?" or something like that. ..... whoever it was stopped. So I thought, to hang with this, so I kept going and then ..... I could see there was a 'T' junction, so I either had to go left or right. And I thought, which way will I go? And I could make out a great big tree on the left, just on the corner. So I thought, I know I'll nip behind the tree and let whoever it is go by, or maybe I'll see who it is. So I just stood behind the tree, and as soon as I did that, I could sense there was something wrong, and the chap shone his torch in my face; a chap with a big rifle, and I could see his uniform .....

Of course, stupidly, I said to him, "Dutch", because we'd thought we could make Holland, you see, and he, "Ja!" and he's still got his big rifle against me. And of course he thought I was saying, "Deutsch", you see. However, at that, he heard the footsteps and of course that alerted him, and, of course, he roared out a challenge and a woman answered him. This was this lady going home, or whatever, on her own and didn't want, maybe, to overtake whoever was walking in front of her. So, he called to her and she came over, and he quickly searched me and I can remember I had a bar of chocolate in my jacket, which went into his pocket and I think I had an orange. We were very fortunate to get anything like that, and he gave the orange to this lady, and she then went off, obviously, to round up the locals and it wasn't long, we were quite close to another village or it might have been, I might have walked in a circle, I don't know.

Albert was transported to Dulag Luft near Frankfurt. Nearly all captured Allied airmen were sent there to be interrogated before being assigned to a permanent prison camp, which in Albert's case was Stalag IVB very early in 1944.

..... we were marched, or taken by this funny wee train, and then marched down to the Frankfurt, sort of, goods yard, and they had wagons there which were used for carrying horses and that, I think, and there was 80 of us put into one of these. And there was barely room, well you couldn't all lie down, you could just about sit down, that was all, and that was it. And we were, I think it was two nights and three days travelling across Germany, being shunted here there and everywhere and we got virtually no food and we arrived at the Stalag, Stalag IVB, which was about 20 miles west of Dresden, on the Elbe. ..... We got out and we'd to walk up the road. There was about six inches of snow and slush on the road and the camp looked dreadful, like, pitch dark, horrible night, snow and slush on the ground, and just the towers, with the searchlights on them, that you could see in the camp. And all we could see were people lining the wire as it were, and shouting at us, but you couldn't make out what was being said, we were too far away. So, anyway, when we arrived, we were taken to, what they called, the de-lousing place, because, none of us had washed, we were in this horrible train thing, wagon, and we were shown in, told, "Strip!" and that meant, literally, you took every scrap off, hung your clothes on a hanger. And of course, I had flying boots, and your shoes, boots, whatever, and it was all put in, or onto, a trolley thing which was shoved into a room and it was treated with some sort of chemical; absolutely ponged when you got your clothes back, but the idea was it killed any bugs or that, that you had.

Albert's PoW photo, taken by his German captors.

..... [My mother had received a telegram] on the day after, on the 30th [December 1943], she had a telegram and the post office, or whoever it was, postman, or whatever that delivered was sensible enough. My father, at that time, he worked in the oil cake mills; he was a foreman there, and the postie knew him, and took it there. So my father, then, had to break the news to my mother, that I was missing, that's what they said, and then it was [well into 1944] before they knew that I was a prisoner of war. ..... and it was the end of May, before I knew that they knew!

..... you were given two, like an airmail-type letter, and, you got two of these, and two postcards a month to write. Course there was chaps who didn't write to anybody, for whatever reason, you could always get extra ones, and it worked very well.

..... I think, probably, being ill, really ill, was a concern. Fortunately, we were all very fit; *very* fit, I think.

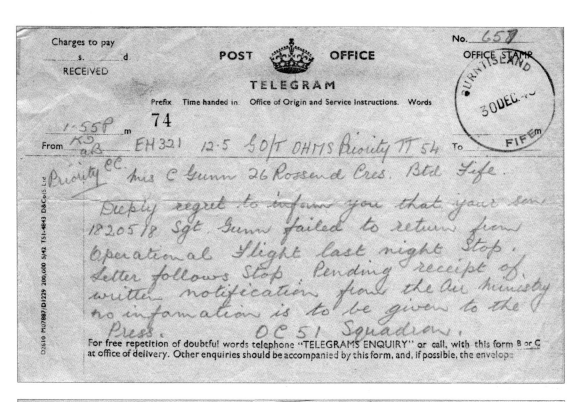

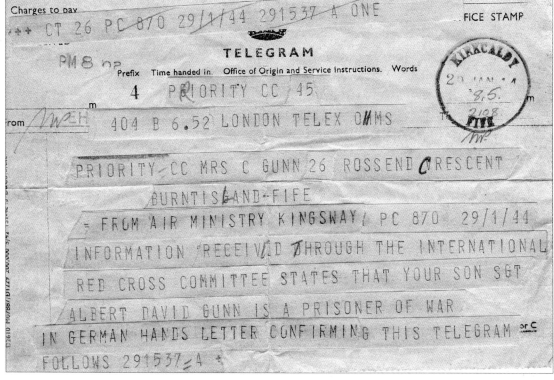

The two telegrams received by Albert's parents in Burntisland - the top one reporting him missing at the end of December 1943, and the bottom one confirming at the end of January 1944 that he was a prisoner of war. Albert Gunn collection.

interieur van een der ...

And I suppose it's a silly thing, but you don't notice how you're doing but you're watching the other ones and you look at them, and you think, crikey, they're losing weight. ..... I was eleven stone ..... when I was in the R.A.F. at that time, you know when we were in operations. ..... Just under seven stone when I came home.

..... you had to adapt to eat what came. And a lot of it was very unappetising and what have you, but this particular night I went to bed and I gone to sleep, woke up and I thought, I feel awful, I'm going to be sick. And we were at one end of the hut, actually, I've got a photograph of a typical hut. What you had, was, two of these huts, wooden huts and they were divided, kept apart, by a stone built part which was a wash house place, and really all it was, was concrete troughs with cold water taps. ..... there was a small toilet, and I thought, I was at this end of the hut, so I thought, I'll never make it. ..... I'll be sick all over the floor, so I just got up and headed for this wash house, unaware that the drain had been blocked and there was about six inches of water with some ice on top of it, out in this place. And I remember standing there and being really sick; I really felt awful. And that's the last time I was sick or ill or anything at all, until VE Day, the 8th of May '45.

..... [There was a] brick built [oven] and you've just got a hot plate on top, and you've got another one there, and they're linked to a central chimney. ..... that's where a hundred people cooked every day, if they had anything to cook, or to heat up. ..... And also, the thing was, that you couldn't all cook or heat anything up at the same time, because you didn't have the utensils to do it with. It was a case of borrowing and people borrowed.

..... The German diet was once a day. When we were at Dulag Luft, where we first started, and this chap said you will get your lovely breakfast in the morning, all you heard was this barrow coming along the corridor, with squeaky wheels and it would stop outside your door, and the chap opened it and if you were quick enough, you could get him to hand you the two slices of black bread stuck together with, they reckoned it was a jam that was made from beetroot. The Germans had a lot of things like that, that they made, you know 'ersatz' as they called it, but it was just something that stuck the bread together, and you got like a wee nip, glass of whisky, but it was black coffee you got, and their coffee, they reckoned, was made from acorns, and it was absolutely foul and I still couldn't face any of that. The bread, I tried to eat, and at the Dulag Luft, I mean, it was still just two or three days, obviously, since we'd been shot down, I used the coffee to sprinkle on the floor to keep the dust down, because I'd tried exercising, just for something to do, there was nothing else to do.

Albert remained in Stalag IVB until April 1945, when he and the other prisoners were liberated by Soviet troops.

..... we got into April and we knew, it was a question of would the Americans or the British get to us, or would the Russians? And time went on, the odds were pretty well it was going to be the Russians, and, of course, we didn't know ..... that at Yalta, Churchill and Roosevelt and Stalin had divvied the whole place up anyway, and that the Russians would come as far as the Elbe, and stop, and the Americans would be opposite us, but they left an 18 mile gap between the two. However, we were on the Elbe, but we were on the East side of the Elbe, which was the Russian part. Anyway, things carried on, and of course, what happened in April was that the American Air Force were operating over our area, and from morning till night there was aircraft

On the opposite page - three photographs of Stalag IVB, where Albert was a prisoner of war. Top - the de-lousing chamber. Middle - the interior of a typical hut as described by Albert in his reminiscences. Bottom - one of the six guard towers, which would normally be manned by two guards with machine guns. Albert Gunn collection.

about. ..... They went for everything that moved. And we'd had a working party out gathering, there was woods and that, they used to be knocking down trees; the branches and everything we were allowed to bring in for firewood for cooking. And a group had been out, had stopped outside the camp with the guards for a rest and for the guards, also I think, to count them all, make sure they were bringing them all back, when these two American Mustangs came over. And I, that day, had been duty cook, but I couldn't get anything done because there was a Russian prisoner of war was re-pointing a lot of the chimney, which was leaking, and so we were waiting on him finishing. So I was lying on the bunk and reading, when we heard this aircraft diving and then suddenly it opened up, firing, and then zoomed off. And next thing we heard another one, and I just bailed out from, we were in the middle bunk, onto the floor, a brick floor and a load of other chaps who had been in the same situation all bailed out as well, but I was on the bottom. I was lying there and I suddenly felt myself getting all wet round the stomach and that, and I thought, crikey, I feel all right, apart from all these heroes on top of me. Of course, what had happened was somebody had kicked the prisoner of war bucket over, ... we were lying in the water. But we had chaps killed in the hut.

Actually, the bunk we were in got hit as well. There were five people killed and a number injured there. But that went on, we saw Thunderbolts shooting up an ammunition train, blowing it to smithereens. I saw, probably one of the first jets, a Messerschmitt 262 being shot down, just outside the camp, by a Thunderbolt. Mind you, it was an easy one because, I think, the German was on one engine, the other one was smoking badly. And the Thunderbolt caught him ..... there was an airfield just a few miles away, he was on his approach to land, poor chap. Flying Fortresses we saw bombing the airfield and all this activity, then it went quiet.

And on, I think it was the 22nd of April, we woke up and somebody said, "The Russians are here." We all dived out, and coming up the, sort of, main, straight road was this bloke on horseback, one bloke, and he came in the gate. And, of course, the guards gone, no guards or anything ..... they went in the night, and some of the chaps saw most of them when they went out on the search for food, hanging in the trees. The Russians had hung them all. They'd surrounded the camp that night, the night before and all the guards got strung up, which was a shame. They didn't deserve it, some of them.

..... We were there for two weeks, I think it was, and it was getting worse and worse; there was no rations at all. If you had to eat you had to find it yourself, and, eventually, one Sunday, we were ordered on parade and we went out and we walked, we think, between 25 and 30 mile, from Muleberg you know, the village, or where the camp was, right down the Elbe. We crossed the Elbe at a place called Strehle - there was a pontoon bridge the Russians had put up - and down to this town, Riesa. It was a town the size of Kirkcaldy maybe, about 60,000 population. That had been the headquarters of a Panzer division, workshops and all that. The Russians stripped it, every nut and bolt to take back to Russia. And we found it incredible as we walked into Riesa, in the evening, we'd walked most of the day, and German ladies were coming out with trays of drinks for us, soft drinks and that. We couldn't, we thought, crikey, we're supposed to be the hated ones, but they were fly, they knew, they'd already sussed that if there was an American/British bloke in the house, Russians wouldn't come in. The Russians were very wary of us, they disliked us for a start, but very wary. So, five of us, we peeled off and went into this nice house and there was this lady with a daughter who was handicapped, severely handicapped, mentally, I think. None of them could speak English and, of course, we could speak less German apart from the swear words we got to know. And we used to go out looking for food and she used to prepare and cook it. But that only lasted a few days and then the Russians brought in a regiment, I suppose you'd call them. They'd a green band round their hat. They were, I think, a sort of police, some type of police. And they took control, controlled traffic, controlled everything, and they controlled us. We were ordered into the Panzer place, barracks and they put a guard on. We could still get out, but nonetheless ..... we never really got comfortable with the

Russians at all. And then we were told one day, "You're moving." And we'd been told that a few times, but this time it was right. Again, it coincided with pouring rain and we marched out of the town to a big field and we waited there, and then a stream of lorries arrived. This was the Americans bringing, whatever they were, Russian slave workers or that back from their side and we all piled on the lorries, onto an autobahn and we went to Halle near Leipzig. .....

I think it was a couple of days later, about a hundred Dakotas flew into the airfield. It was actually on a base, an airfield. It had been an airfield where the Germans did a lot of experimental flying and that. There was a lot of odd aircraft about, but anyway, these Dakotas came in and we flew on a Friday, it was to Brussels, and we were taken and put in a hostel and I can see it yet, this lovely bed - nice single bed - with *white* sheets on it. And we were handed £10 in Belgian money and we were told, in Belgium they have wee tramcar things running up, and anybody in uniform, you just got on, and we said, "Right." We were off.

..... So the next morning, or actually that same morning, I should say, it was Saturday morning by then, we were very tired and weary, because we hadn't been to bed and we were taken out to the airfield in Brussels.

Albert was flown to Oakley in Oxfordshire in a Lancaster bomber.

..... the first thing they gave us, I think at Wolverhampton, was a telegram form, and I just put on it, "Arrived in England, be home soon," something like that and then sent it off.

..... they hadn't got the telegram ..... by the time I got home and, as I say, I came off the train, going up to the Castle and I was walking up, towards the arches and I remember Bunty Couser was coming down the road and she worked at Donibristle and she said to me, "What are you doing here?" I said, "Well, I'm on my way home." She said, "But they're not expecting you." I said, "Well, I'm sorry about that, but I'm still going home." And that was it, I just walked up [to our house in Shepherd Crescent] and, as I say, my mother had a routine, she used to do all her front door brasses first thing, and that, because when I walked in the path, I could see them all shining. I thought, oh she's done that bit; she'll be in the kitchen, probably. So I walked round, knocked and opened the kitchen door and she was in the lounge, actually, cleaning out or setting the fire and she just looked up and said, "Oh, I thought it'd be you." So I said to her, "Oh, you got the telegram?" "Oh, what telegram? No." ..... [I hadn't seen her since] 18th December '43. ..... Eighteen months.

Oh, I was whacked and I went to bed, but like Burntisland, well even more so in those days, everything went round like wildfire and the door bell would ring and folk were saying, "Is it right he's home?" and mother was saying, "Yes," and I'm trying to sleep. "Oh can we see him?" "He's in his bed." "Yes, but we could just peep and see he's there," or whatever, and they'd come creaking up the stairs and you're trying to kid on you're asleep

..... I got up in the afternoon and there was all this activity downstairs and they're making up sandwiches and cakes been done and all the rest of it, and I said, "What on earth's this for?" "Oh, well, it's welcome home," but I said, "How?" She said, "There'll be something on tonight," ..... and my sister-in-law, Margaret, was there and so about seven o'clock, up comes the pipe band. Hundreds of folk outside and a banner up, and welcome home, and out I went and I got handed £40, which was a lot of money. They'd had a whip-round all round, you know, the neighbours.

And then there was dancing on the street. And it was quite funny because I stood with Margaret, my sister-in-law, and the band's playing away and I said, "Why isn't folk dancing?" "Well," she said, "they're waiting for you to lead it off." I thought, oh crikey!

Jimmy Wilson's Story

*Jimmy (on the right),
pictured in Rome.*

1940 comes along, I was called up. I did my army trainin g in Elgin. Royal Engineers. 6th Battalion of the Training Battalion, Royal Engineers. I did twelve weeks in Elgin, training, posted to my first unit in Tunbridge Wells.

..... we did a job in Dover. We put in, well Costain built the gun pits and we put in the rails and the bits for the nine inch guns to fire across the Channel. And there was a bloke, who lives in Burntisland now, stays, belongs to Dover and I spoke to him one time. ..... we were speaking and I found out that he came from Dover and I told him where I had worked and what we had done in St. Margaret's Bay, in Dover. He says, "It wisnae you that put the guns in at Dover, was it?" I says, "Aye it was, I helped them put them in." He says, "You know what happened to them when they first fired?" I says, "No." He says, "They blew all the tiles off the houses down below!" 'Cause St. Margaret's Bay was up high and Dover was away down below.

They did fire them across the Channel, but Jerry fired them across the Channel an a'. Jerry fired one day; when Costain's foreman blew his whistle for the men to start work, the first shell landed in the Duke o' York's school, which was opposite St. Margaret's Bay and the golf course. And when the foreman blew his whistle to stop at dinnertime, Jerry stopped, and he started again when the foreman blew his whistle to start. And all he knocked down in that 8 hours of shelling was 100 yards of railing, never killed anybody, never hit anything, just a railing.

But the next week, there was a football match on in Dover and he sent a couple of shells across and one landed in the centre of the football park, and there was lots of them killed and some of them wouded and different things .....

..... some of [the Burntisland lads] went to the merchant navy, even before the war. Some of them joined up the Royal Navy before the war. Some of them joined the Army before the war, but they were a' servicemen, they a' joined, they were a' in it during the war, the Royal Navy, merchant navy.

..... there was one bloke, you'll maybe no' know him, he used to go round collecting bottles oot the buckets and different things like that, he was torpedoed three times. He joined the Navy 1932, '33, something like that, he joined the Navy, but he got oot though ..... I don't think he ever worked after he came out the Navy, because ..... he wisnae right.

Yes, I went abroad, I was posted from Tunbridge Wells ..... down to Halifax in Yorkshire, and I went from there, I joined the SS Laconia, or Motor Vessel Laconia, and we sailed from Southampton to Greenock, and from Greenock to the Middle East and we stopped once at Freetown. And then from Freetown we sailed right through to Egypt and then went to a base camp called Moasker, and from there I went up the desert to Tobruk .....

I was taken prisoner at Tobruk 12th May 1942 ..... we were out working in the desert, doing, I canna'+ mind, it was something to do wi' water we were doing and we had stopped and this bloody daft English officer saw this crowd o' men away down in the distance and he says, "Oh, there's a Union Jack flying down there," and somebody turned round and said, "That's not a Union Jack, that's a bloody Swastika," and it was ..... the Germans. And they came up, right up to us, and the first thing they did, was take your rifle away and break the butt off it, and they just threw you in the back o' a wagon and took you away. And we stopped, oh, I canna mind the name o' the place, anyway, we stopped, but our own blokes was shelling us, and we were a' in shell holes and getting covered up ..... And two tanks came through and you never seen anybody getting off their mark as quick as these Germans when the tanks started to come through, but they went away and they left a three-ton lorry, couldnae get it started. So ..... we got it started and went on the three ton lorry. Went back towards Tobruk and we landed on a minefield, we blew the wheels off the truck.

Inside the truck there was about twenty-four ..... North Africans, there was about the same number of British troops ..... and we landed on this minefield and the North Africans, they all jumped out the truck and got her out, along, round the side, never stepped on a mine, walked through the minefield. Then we shouted them back, they came back, and we got round and we walked away and ..... landed in an Indian camp. And it was getting night time, getting on for night in the Indian camp, and we a' settled down. I settled down in a big shell hole an' a big stone for a pillow. Took my boots off and fell asleep. The next thing I remember was a wee Indian shaking me wi' a mug o' tea and a packet o' Woodbine cigarettes and a box o' matches. [We] had to go in front of their officer, who was an Englishman, and then we were posted back to our own units.

But that is when the trouble started, because we were chased back to Cairo. ..... one day I'd lost a' my gear ..... I lost everything. I lost my clothes, everything that I had, unless I was carrying it wi' me. .....

And we had this silly parade in this big compound in Cairo, and because I had no cleaning materials, well, you'll maybe have minded o' soldiers wi' a forage cap, one o' these things. I had one, a forage cap, and my buttons were dirty, two buttons on the front, and when the Sergeant Major and the officer came down, they looked at me and they said, "Why is your buttons not clean?" I says, "I haven't got any cleaning materials." "Why?" I told them why, they knew why, but I told them again. They said, "Why didn't you borrow cleaning materials?" They asked me the number o' my tent where I was. ..... I was put on a charge for having two dirty buttons on my forage cap. After I'd been taken prisoner and that. I was put on a charge and I went in front o' the Captain o' the unit, and he went through all the rigmarole. ..... And he just looked at me, he says, "You accept my punishment?" I says, "Yes, sir." One day's pay stopped!

..... Jerry came back, shoved us back to Cairo but we then worked our way back, and that was when we were out in the desert. And that was when Montgomery was sorting out El Alamein, and went from there right through. And after that it was easy, well, it wisna' easy, but we never had any more trouble after that. [We were] maybe picking up mines or laying mines, whatever was necessary. It wisnae until ye come further, ye went through the desert into Italy that you had to start building bridges and things like that.

..... I landed at Salerno. We went right up through Italy. I had fourteen days leave in Rome. Been in Florence, and Naples. ..... And we ..... picked up this wee Italian, an Italian prisoner, took him wi' us and he worked in the cookhouse and he worked round about. His name was Alfredo Tamborelli .....

Anyway, we were in this factory, the acetylene, where we used to sell petrol. We had customers outside in the village. And I was out one night and I found, oh, about 200 fifty gallon drums and I wondered what was in them. And I got this Alfredo Tamborelli to come out with me, and unscrewed the top and in these drums, in these fifty gallon drums, was Italian cooking fat, so when we went out in my mate's lorry at night, that's what we had in the lorry, Italian cooking oil, acetylene and petrol! I never drew ..... a pay out my pay book a' the time I was in Italy!

..... Alfredo could speak Italian. He was Italian and a good lad, he was a good lad, a welder to trade, an electric welder ..... I mind one day, we went to Florence, a day off, we had a day off or something.

Above - the Royal Engineers unit of the British Eighth Army, photographed in Italy in 1944. Jimmy Wilson is in the front row, third from the left. Jimmy Wilson collection.

After the war, Jimmy returned to his old job at the aluminium works. In 1949 he moved to Fisons in Lothian Street. Jimmy and his sister are pictured (left) outside the Fisons works. The photograph was taken around 1959, when Jimmy was works foreman. Jimmy Wilson collection.

We saw this shop, and it was in this shop, a white silk scarf, and why I wanted it, I'll never know ..... and we were in the shop and spoke to the Italian and whatever, and he was gonna charge me an enormous amount of money to buy this white silk scarf and Alfredo came in and you shoulda seen this, eh? He nearly went mad when he asked what I was gonna pay for it and I told him. And he turned round and he said to the Italian, "You," he says, "these men have saved your life ....." I got the scarf for nothing! I don't know where it went or what I did wi' it, but it wisnae any use to me, but it was just something I saw and I wanted. But Alfredo was a good lad; he was a nice bloke.

~ ~ ~ ~ ~

..... even in Germany, everybody was at it. I mean I came home on leave once, my mother and sister had stayed in Edinburgh during the war, 'cause my sister was working in Edinburgh during the war, and I came home on leave and I was ready to go back, in fact, I was going back that night, and I went out wi' my mother, she was going out shopping. ..... That would be ..... just before I came out the army, 1945, roond about that time, '46 maybe, just before I came out. And when I went into the shop, a grocer's shop wi' my mother, it was up Lauriston Place, this bloke says to me, "Are you home on leave?" I says, "I've been, I'm going back the night." He said, "You'll be taking coffee back wie ye," and I thought, bloody hell, what am I gonna do [with that], and then it suddenly dawned on me, aye I could take a bag, so I took seven pounds o' coffee back to Germany and flogged it in Germany .....

I hadnae that long to go, anyway, I had another leave to get ..... and I went in to see the officer and he said, "Well, this'll be the last leave you get, Wilson." He says, "If you can make enough money, the same as in your pay book, ... we'll pay you in postal orders and when you come out, when you get out, you change the postal orders." So that was what we did ..... Postal orders, we changed them when I came home on leave. And ..... everybody was at it, even the officers were at it.

Rolf Rademacher's Story

Rolf was born in 1926 in Wuppartal, Germany. He joined the German Navy when he was sixteen years old.

I was in the Navy. What happened, I wanted to go in the Navy, like, but I was sixteen years old and my faither wouldn't ..... ken, the only way you could get in, you have to volunteer for it, well when I was waiting, I had a year, they just shoved you in the Army and I didn't want that, but my faither wouldn't bloomin' sign the papers for me going in there. So I got my mate to sign my faither's name and I changed my date of birth, and that's the way I got in.

I was about sixteen and a half, but you had to be seventeen. See in the German Navy, ... they used to have the cadets in Germany, the same as what they have here, but it was no' necessary you had to go in. I mean I'm being honest about it ..... with the Brownshirts and that. If I had put a brown shirt on, my faither would have killed me. My old man was the biggest Communist in the country, and he didn't like [the Brownshirts.] See he lost his business and everything, my faither. See, the Nazi party asked him to bloomin' print stuff for them, my faither was a printer, and they wanted him to print leaflets and stuff like that, and my old man refused. They starved him out; so he had to pay the men off and eventually he had to flog all the machinery and that, ken? I mean, just before the War started, and my old man ..... somebody seen him with a briefcase and [alleged it contained Communist leaflets] ..... well that my old man didn't do. ..... he was maybe a Communist, but the minute Hitler got on the government, he stopped his activities. He didn't bother with it. But they took him away. Oh, the Gestapo came up to my parents' hoose. They ransacked the hoose, ripped everything apart, the bed, mattress, everything. The hoose was worse than a bloomin' tip. I've seen a tip cleaner than what my mother's hoose was. They ripped the place up looking for leaflets.

..... So they took him away with them ..... He was away for about four hours, or something like that, I canny actually mind aboot it, and they come back ..... my father stopped the activity anyway. I mind I had an uncle, ... he couldn't fling his arm high enough. Him and my faither, when they see each other, they spit at each other's face. And then after the war they was ..... they was the best of pals. I don't know why! That's the way life goes.

..... When I joined the Navy, actually what happened, I managed to pick up the call-up papers. I managed to get the postie. So I had a look at it on the fly, and nobody was [any the wiser.] I did take it up to the hoose and read it and I just put it in my pocket. And so I come hame and I start packing my case. My Mum says, "Where are you going?" I says, "I'm going away camping wi' the boys." She says, "You've just had your holidays." ..... so I buggered off!

..... I joined up. I was up at Kiel ..... And then we got sent to Denmark as training, ken, Army training for six weeks. And I came back from the training from Denmark ..... I just went as an ordinary seaman at the time, ken. And then I went to Kiel again and a lot of things to do before you get the ship. And eventually I got on the subs. I went away out on the subs and that ..... and then after I come back, I was away for aboot near four months and I come back and then away back to school. I was just only going out with the subs and back then you go back to school ..... back to training again and then you work yourselves up, ken, the more you train, the higher you can get. And that was it.

And I mean, that was when I got sunk ..... that happened in 1944 sometime, I canny mind exactly the month, like. That much happened since.

..... most of the time you was underwater. Oh we have to surface every so often, ken, and then they cut the compressor off and the air has to get in ..... trying to get the air in, like.

..... that was in mid Atlantic. [Only] fifteen from fifty-five [escaped.] ..... I was on watch at that time. I think the first officer ..... I think he must have been bloomin' deaf or something. I mean I tried to relieve him, I says, "Do you hear the noise?" He said, "What noise?" So I just pressed the things to dive, ken? And that was it and just when I was trying to put the hatch down, I just looked up and I seen the plane, ken, diving. The thing is the sky was not clear at that time and there was just this clear patch and I just seen [it.] So the time I seen it, the pilot must have seen us an' all and they flung a bomb ..... and that was it. There was just only fifteen come out. Fifteen out of fifty-five.

I don't know how long I was in the water and the junks, baskets. I be honest about it, I don't know much about it ..... I mind I got out. I was the first one come out. ..... by the time I got fished oot I was, more or less, half dead. I can't mind ..... how they picked me up, I don't know. I don't know how long I was in the water.

I tell you one thing, you went in the water and you're trying to keep afloat, ... and then your mind it just goes blank. ..... Christ the next thing I was lying on board a ship and these bloomin' ..... took everything, the Yankees took everything what you had on, ken. You had waterproof stuff on, ken, like you had the flotation and so on. I had photos and that from my mother and father and that. Ah, but the Yankees, they just ..... when you tried to pick it up, they just kicked your bloomin' arse. I don't have time for the Yanks.

[I was rescued by] a convoy coming from America going to Britain. ..... I was in Britain for a wee while, then I got shoved to America. And then I come back here .....

I mean, when I was in Germany, I was working in Germany for four years. When you was a Scotsman, you was welcome and then there was an Englishman, "Off! We're no wanting you. Table doon there." When the Scotsman came in they says, "Come on, Jock, here. Sit here." That's how the German people were. They didn't want the English people.

After his rescue and being shuttled to and fro across the Atlantic, Rolf ended up in a prisoner of war camp in Scotland.

That, in some part it was good; in other part it was not. I mean I'm no trying to bloomin' tell you a story aboot it, but in some camps it was all right, it was quite good and that, but in other ones ..... it was not too good either, and you had to watch like a hawk. I mean, I've been in quite a few places, like. I've been up in Stranraer, been north to Wick, ... bloomin' down at Blair Atholl.

..... Aye, that was prisoner of war camps. For a start you wasnae allowed to get out anywhere. You just go to your work and that was it. A lorry picked you up and then they drove you into ..... the farm, wherever you was going. [Farm work was] all I was allowed to do, but I got the chance in '49. See I really got the chance out the prisoner of war camp in '49 ..... I went home [to Germany] in '49, January of '49. I was going to Munster in Westphalia and that's where all the prisoners [were] discharged. ..... you got fourteen marks, fourteen marks at that time, you couldn't buy really anything for it. The money wasnae worth it. There was no work in Germany, anyway, and that's why I come back.

..... the time I was in the prisoner of war camp, they had the prisoners in three groups, 'A', 'B' and 'C'. 'A' was the Democrats, 'B' was the people, like o' my age, they was non-political. ..... the 'C' was the Nazis, ... the bloomin' biggest Nazis in the world. ..... 'A', that was the Democrats, ... they was the first to go home back to Germany, but they [included some of the worst] Nazis ..... They couldn't fling their arms high enough. .....

..... I mean we had ..... he was the biggest Nazi, and he was an SS person. He was pretty high up. He was the first ane got hame, but what happened, but he got warned. He [was told,] "You go hame, you'll no last very long." He got home ..... He got discharged out the camp in Munster. He never sees his hometown. He was out the camp and [the local people] killed him there. ..... Aye, oh they killed him the minute he ..... walked oot the gate. That was in Germany.

..... So the way I looked at it, most of them Democrats, I would say about seventy per cent of them was bloomin' Nazis; they got home first. And then the real Democrats, they was [also] going home first. [But] the like o' us, we wasnae allowed the vote at that time to get Hitler and the government, we got put doon as a Nazi. I was supposed to be the bloomin' 'C', a super Nazi and I never [was] ..... I've never been in the Brownshirts or nothing. I just was only in the Navy, ken? And that's what I couldn't understand. ..... We was the last ones to go hame. .....

They asked you a lot of questions and at the time I wisnae sure and that was before I found oot my parents were still alive. I mean I just only knew about it in 1948, that my mother and father was still alive. They was in the same street, the same house, they never moved. And all the letters I had sent, they was going through the Red Cross in Switzerland, but they never got the letters. And they just had only one letter all the time I was in the prisoner of war camp, and my Mother wrote and that letter went away for about 18 months before it reached me. .....

I signed a [British work] contract in '48 and the British government would send us home for six weeks for a holiday, and they paid the fare coming back. ..... my mother didn't want me to go back, but I says, "I signed the contract, and I'll stick by it."

Having signed the work contract before his release in 1949, Rolf returned to Scotland after six weeks in Germany.

After I got to Dundee, so I was on the farm up to 1950. ..... Oh, no, [I didn't find much anti-German feeling,] but I mean, you see, we hardly managed to get out. I got on well with everybody. ..... I was pretty much well liked and I got on with them all, like. ..... And I used to go doon the pub and a lot o' the ploughmen was there and that, ken. And they said, "What aboot coming to the old Palais?" Ken, that was the Scottish dancing. I says, "Aye," I mind there was a ..... boy, a workman, his girlfriend, he says, "Come on, I'll learn you to dance." And I mean I was half chackit, like, ken? And I just ..... I danced the Scottish so much and then I was getting fed up and then I start bloomin' diving under, and he says, "Look at that silly bugger." See a couple o' years after they all bloomin' da'in' that; they still doing it yet. I started before that ever came out. And they used to say, "Look at that stupid bugger." That was some laugh.

I got married in December 1950. I couldn't get [married accommodation] so I had to come off the farm, so I didn't know ..... I just walking about, out and in, ask permission. I had to ask permission if I can walk anywhere, ken, and I explained to them. So I got permission from the Home Office, and I could take any job. So I walked away round different places. I mean Dundee was full of jute mills and all that.

..... Well I moved away from one farm to the other. I was in Angus. Oh, I was in Crieff, in a dairy farm in Crieff. But I was married by that time, and I was in Forfar, I was travelling quite a lot, like. I seen quite a lot of the country. I'm just trying to ..... I canna mind ..... I'm just trying to remember, I was in Howie, the Grange, I started working in there in 1955, I think it was '55. I was in Howie's hoose for six months ..... I didn't dae a year, ken? ..... you have to stay a year. When you don't they bloomin' ..... they take the money off you for the flitting. So I was just only six months with Howie. The Grange, you ken when you go to Kirkcaldy? And when you come out of Kinghorn, you go doon the hill, it's on the left hand side. .....

..... I was in Blairgowrie, I come doon, and that's where I came from to go into ..... come into Fife and I worked doon there for six months and there was a woman, she came from Kinghorn and she was telling me there was a job in Fison's [in Burntisland.] So I went away doon and had an interview and it was just aboot a month before the summertime, ken, where they go on holiday, so I got the [job].

..... So I flitted on the Friday, I got a house from Fison's and I was just on Lothian Street there. ..... it was a two bedroom, ken, but I had four kids. I mean that was better, get away from the farm, like.

..... Fison's? I was with them quite a few years like, but then they closed the place. ..... [Until it closed,] they kept some people on, but what happened, the trade union rules at that time, the last in, first out. So there was somebody came in the back o' me and I was a person longer in there than that boy was, but he was a wee bit of a ..... wi' the manager. He came all the way from Thornton, and I mean, the wages wisna that big and that boy never had any intention to work overtime anyway. He kept the job on; I mean, look at what it cost him for the bus fare all week. And the wages wasna that big. I canna mind, it's about four pound ten or something at that time. That was in 1956. ..... they closed down after that. It was about '58. ..... they used to get the stuff brought in on the cart, ken from the docks ..... it was Wishart, the two brothers, Wishart. They had a business here and the one of them stayed in the Fison building and the other one stayed away up round the back near where the stable was, like.

Rolf has lived in Burntisland ever since.

Bill Stratton's Story

Bill Stratton was born in Poland in 1916. In the Second World War, Germany regarded Gdansk as part of its own territory, i.e. the German city of Danzig.

..... went to high school for four years ..... then I went to a commercial college for three years. And then I was employed by a wholesale grocers, distilleries, you know, and they had a monopoly for vodka, wholesale, all the rest.

[We had conscription] before the war, ... everybody at the age of 21 had to go to the medical ..... I went to the medical in 1937, in January, there was snow lying about, five inches, sort of, we had exercises, all the rest, anyhow. That was a technical company I went to. It belonged to the 16th Division, a division is usually about 20,000 people. We was delegated as a company, separate from the Division, ... signal, company of signal, radio. ..... Morse, all the way, and wireless of course. So I landed there for 20 month, from January '37 till September '38. I was a reservist. Then I went home.

[In 1939] I got marching orders ..... to the Polish Army, to the signals ..... And I was a wireless operator there, and of course, two days later on, the war broke out. We got the first manoeuvres from East Prussia, that the tanks crossed Polish border, that was the first news ..... the division was along the border, like, about 20 kilometres from us, where the wireless station was, headquarters station. So the division ..... were all ready grouped on the East ...... Of course, they were overtaken. I mean there was tanks, tanks and then Stuka bombers, big bombers and night fighters and everything else. I mean it made a mess of everything, wherever it was, it was a free zone, practically, the Germans went through the flanks, never stopping.

So we had to go, on the third day when the War broke out, we got a command to retreat, to Warsaw way ..... we had to go on foot. ..... we had a [horse drawn] wireless station, ... [but] the horses weren't good enough because they couldn't go every day, [just] for a few hours, have to be fed and rest. Anyhow, so we abandoned [it], I just got a wireless station on my back ..... but we didn't get good contact with the frontline people, because it was all destroyed, ... was panic and anyway, so we went back, seventeen days, practically from East Prussian border practically up to Warsaw, from this side of Vistula. And there, of course, we didn't know what was going on, we thought all our soldiers are here so we should get a nice front, against the Germans now. And somebody said, "..... you [have] not a chance to get out." Everything, all the whole Polish Army was surrounded, and then was smaller, and smaller, and smaller. "By the end of it," he said, "you have to get white hankies, whatever." [We had no] chance, because [we were] overwhelmed, power the Germans had, you know.

I was taken prisoner, yes, hands up, of course, looked for whatever we had, like, took everything, papers, everything from us. Then they ask you, "Anybody speak German?" And then well, I said, "Yes." So I translated bits and pieces, whatever I had to do, like, you know. And we got in lorries, German lorries; there was, oh, about a hundred or so lorries with about thirty people, forty people in a lorry, just as we were. Oh but September wasn't too bad [although we were] without food for the last two, three days; nothing to eat, nothing to drink. And we got transported to the Polish barracks ..... about 1,000 kilometres further away. So we stayed there till the end and then ..... after three, four days, I think, we got to know that people [who were] born under German occupation[4] at one time, wherever that was, had a good chance to get home. And that's what happened. I was married in 1939, in May, and in September 1939, you know, I was a prisoner of war by the Germans!

..... of course, we had news. ..... I had a wireless in the attic. And I listened to 'London Calling'! ..... I could have been back in jail, I think, if they got me, anyhow. So ..... say, nine, ten o'clock, went upstair, like, and my wife even didn't know. I didn't want to involve her, in case something would have happened to her, like, and children, eventually ..... And I listened, knew what was [happening], and that what made me later on go to France, because I got all the news from London through Polish stations, in Poland, like, you know. And Warsaw, of course, the underground, 'Warsaw Calling', as well, it was a Polish news, for Poles abroad, in Poland, under occupation and all, encouraging anybody to destroy whatever ability the Germans had, railway stations, factories, sabotage this, sabotage that, kill Germans and the rest of it.

..... We got from a Polish wireless, from Warsaw, we didn't know where it was, Warsaw, wherever it was in Poland, calling all ex-servicemen Poles to unite and if you have a chance, to go to France ..... Brest I think it was, near the channel. [In] 1944. ..... [I told my wife] they can help us, because we didn't know if we would stay where we were, with the business and everything else, because Hitler was killing left and right people, arresting people and the rest and they had to prove that you were [of the] Aryan Race and all that ..... and I told her, "Well, I just go to France to see," you know, I didn't tell her that I was in an underground, she didn't know

---

[4] This refers to the German occupation of areas of Poland in the period 1871 to 1919. These areas were returned to Poland under the Treaty of Versailles of 1919, and re-occupied by Germany in 1939.

that, like.

..... I just went with essentials and went to Paris, to Paris first, the Gare du Nord. ..... I had identity card, and we were going back and forward, we could go to Germany, anytime, with the German identity card, like. So, that was no problem, I spoke German, they wouldn't have taken me for a Pole or for anybody else, because my accent was German, just like a German. So I was just lucky enough, I could travel in Germany and nobody would have noticed ..... there were a lot of Germans in France. Oh, there were soldiers, of course, like everybody else, but the Germans had spies and everything else, but I managed, landed in Paris ..... I got a ticket to Brest, Brest to the Channel Islands, you know. I managed to get there no bother, and then I got in contact, there are places in Brest and they asked me, "What do you do?" I says, "Oh, I was a prisoner of war ..... and I'm still active as a Pole. I wouldn't mind if I joined the Polish Army." ..... He gave me an address and everything else, he said, "We are organising just now," he says, "We have nothing concrete to get you over to Britain, so we are waiting first a ship to take all those who volunteer and want to go to Britain and, like you, want to go to Polish Army, we will have a date for that."

..... we went to Britain with a ship to Southampton ..... so I landed with a group when we went to Southampton, from Southampton to a British [camp.] There was military police, I think it must have been, didn't know the British Army. Anyhow, I think it was a British police, military police, like, and [they] asked us questions ..... they asked me, "You speak German?" "Yes," I says, "I speak French as well," I said, you know. "Oh," he said, "we need a man like you," he says! .....

[The Polish army] were based in Falkirk, 1st Division. ..... where the teacher training college is now, I think it was.

Bill served with the Polish Army until the war ended. His ability to speak Polish, German, French, and a little Russian - but initially not much English! - was invaluable, and he often acted as a translator. However, it was not until 1945 that his mother and wife were able to get confirmation that he was alive and well.

[In 1945] my mother wrote to the Red Cross ..... And then I wrote too, it was allowed from Scotland to write to Poland when the war was finished. ..... And then my mother got [the] letter from me, she says, "Oh, Bill is alive! ..... he's in Scotland in the Polish Army." So my wife got to know that, "Hooray, hooray!" That was a celebration like anything, the kids as well. ..... For Christmas [1946] I went to see my wife and my children. Everybody that was serving in the Polish Army during the War .....had a chance to bring, go home, or bring family over. And then I wrote to my wife ..... saying, "Would you like to come with the children to Scotland? It's a lovely country, there's nothing destroyed," I says. "I speak English now, too," I says, "I can maybe get a job, and maybe our future will be better than you have ..... now."

..... [My brother in law told me about] the order already from authorities in ..... the Gdansk area. ..... children have to be evacuated ..... before the Russians come, you see, because they take children to Siberia. ..... So my brother-in-law, my wife's brother asked my wife and the children, said, "You want to come with me, manage to get somewhere to live ..... in West Germany," so she packed up, go to the bank, even, got some money for maybe two, three days, whatever it was, and she packed up and went with him. ..... she landed in a wee town, it was Koenigslutter ..... and the authorities took over her and the two children ....., they were treated as Germans, German refugees ..... she was getting a room and a kitchen, I think, and there was a toilet outside and the rest. Anyhow, so she got accommodation and ..... social security for the children ..... just escaped from the ..... Russians.

..... And my wife and children were safe, in the West, it was divided, in the Western Germany, like. ..... They were in poor health and the rest of it, but she was alive and the children were alive.

Bill was living in a camp at Kinross at this time, and he asked an official if his wife and children could join him in Scotland.

..... "Oh, yes," he said, "if you have relatives," he said, "on the continent, even in Poland," he says, "You can, it's allowed, you can bring them to where you want to stay for good." ..... So I said, "Yes," and then I got a holiday, went to see them. And then my wife says, "Well, there's no use staying in Germany. We lost everything we had." The Russians emptied everything, the shops, everything, you know.

..... So I got accommodation, two bedrooms in a flat, in a flat in Kinross, through our authorities, you know?

[My wife] knew a wee bit of English, ... better than I did, course I didn't know anything. Anyhow ..... I was still in the Polish Army and went shopping with her and I knew the grocers and post office ..... And then she went eventually by herself for grocers. It was about 200 yards from place where she stayed and the grocers were [in] Kinross. .....

[I left the army] in May 1948. ..... went to the pits. [I was a] miner. ..... I stayed in Kinross, where my wife was, and then in May, there was quite a few, because, as I told you before, there was about 200 officers. They wanted to be resettled, ... to be tailors, or watchmakers, repairers, television repairers, different things, and painters ..... I says, "What use going training for whatever?" I had plenty bits and pieces, in my head, what I wanted to do. And my wife came from business, so she says, "The best way for business, save up and go for the business."

So I joined the mines. It was five pounds fifteen [shillings.] Glencraig pit. ..... I was in Muircockhall, that was outside Dunfermline, for three weeks for training, to see how the mines are, if you like it or not. ..... I was for twelve years a miner. ..... I went for everything that was needed to be a miner in a pit. So I was cutting coal, stripping coal, firing coal, relaying belts, conveyor belts and measuring strippers. How much they have to get out of it and how much it was worth for them every day, whatever. ..... I was the right hand man, you could call it, five star miner. That's what I was.

..... and I got ..... British naturalisation papers.

..... That's twelve years, I was [in the pits.]

..... I was trained a wee bit, and my wife ..... was a teacher, but anyhow, so we thought, business pays better than manual work, you know. It was quite natural. And that's what happened. So we had enough money to buy the wee shop in Burntisland. A very small shop, you know. ..... So I went over there, I never came back. Inside a day, [Mr Brown's] shop was mine. ..... they didn't have much. It was nice and tidy, clean, and they sold coffee, tea, some groceries, and sweets, kids came for sweets and everything. But very limited range, whatever it was, some jigsaws and some postcards, different things like that.

..... Oh, I liked [Burntisland], because it was busy. It was really busy, it was just before Easter I came here, ... and the kids were on the Links, and they were putting, golfing and the swimming pool opened, swimming pool was there and across the road the Ex-servicemen's Club. That was just like a church, back and forward, in and out, in and out, drunks and no drunks ..... The railway station, a school, two churches and the yard, three ships on a keel, was about 2,000 people working there as well. ..... And then the picture house, of course, was there, as well. So there it was, impressed me, really impressed me. Burntisland was really a place which we could settle down here.

Bill, now retired, still lives in Burntisland.

Chapter 4

The Binn Village

Today, as you pass alongside Burntisland golf course on the way to Kinghorn Loch, it is very difficult to envisage the vast industrial undertaking which for a relatively short period - 16 years - dominated the area on the other side of the road. This was the Burntisland (originally Binnend) Oil Works which, at its peak, gave employment to almost a thousand men.

The Burntisland Oil Works were established in 1878 and closed in 1894. The machinery was dismantled and sold immediately, although it was not until 1905 that the land was sold - first to the Whinnyhall Estate Company, and by them to the British Aluminium Company.

While the shale oil works at Binnend are largely forgotten, the village which was built to serve them is not. The building of the village was part of the general expansion following the change of ownership of the oil works in 1881. The village was in fact in two parts - the High Binn at the old Binnend Farm, and the Low Binn close to the main road and east of the oil works. It is likely that both parts of the village were built around the same time, although it is the High Binn whose memory lives on, and to which people are generally referring when they speak of the 'Binn Village'.

Census returns show that the High Binn had a population of 564 in 1891, crammed into 95, mainly two roomed, houses. The population of the Low Binn was 192, in 33 houses. Overall, thirty per cent of the heads of household were Irish, with most of the rest born in Fife or the Lothian shale mining areas. Some of the houses were so overcrowded that the beds were used on a shift system, 24 hours a day; and some slept in the space between the ceiling and the roof.

In 1889, the High Binn acquired a Free Church Mission Hall, which seems to have served all denominations; and in 1891 it got its own school. At that time, there were around 170 children of school age. The village had a football pitch, nestling at the foot of a shale bing, and home to the Binnend Rangers.

There were two small shops in the village, but the inhabitants went to Burntisland for most of their messages. Those of the shale workers who had come from Broxburn and West Calder had brought with them the principle of co-operation, and they were the driving force behind the establishment of Burntisland's first Co-operative store in Harbour Place, which opened in 1884.

When the oil works employees were paid off in 1893, Binnend village remained a going concern, although its permanent population began to decline.

There was a brief revival during the First World War, when troops and dockyard workers occupied houses and the school. And when the aluminium works and the shipyard opened in Burntisland around the end of that war, the village provided good low cost homes for a number of the incoming workers.

In the inter-war years, the decline in the permanent population continued. But many of the houses found a new role as holiday homes for folk from Edinburgh, Glasgow and other parts of Scotland. Basic they might have been, but visitors from the cities loved the fresh air and freedom. The large number of Binn village postcards from that time are now invaluable as a permanent historical record of a lost village.

The absence of basic facilities led to the formal closure of the village about 1931, although some residents insisted on staying on, despite the lack of piped water, gas, electricity and sanitation.

By 1952, only two couples, the Hoods and the McLarens, remained. Early in 1954, the last inhabitant[1], 74 year old George Hood of number 133 High Binn, departed. The village was left to the mercy of the Territorial Army, Alcan Chemicals, the weather and the vegetation. Today very little remains of what was once a thriving settlement.

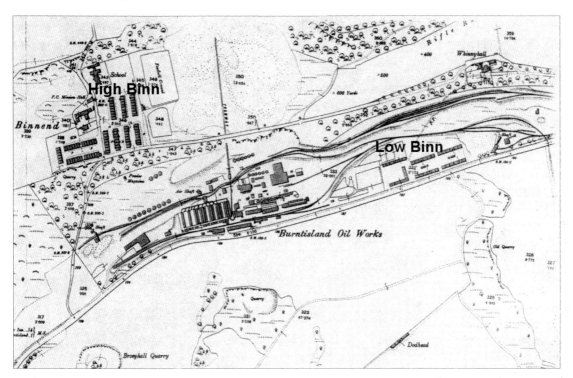

The High Binn and the Low Binn are both marked on this old map, which dates from the days when the oil works were fully developed. The main road from Burntisland to Kinghorn Loch passes just to the south of the oil works and the Low Binn, and follows the same line today. The railway which served the oil works ran from Kinghorn. BHT collection.

Jean Carabine remembers life in the Binn Village:

Oh, we had a shop. Miss Murray had a shop, that she sort o' lay along the counter. And very, very clarty in all sorts o' ways, but we all survived it. She ..... had a machine that she never cleaned.

Vans came around for selling the bread, and the Co-op van and the coal came. The coal was pretty yuch. There was little doors in a wall and behind the wall was a bit space and they emptied it in there. If you wanted more than one bag you got in a hell of a mess!

Aye, we had a coal fire; we had to cook on that. We got a bit richer and got a sort of oil stove, that everybody was really afraid of. And ..... when I think of it, you experienced everything, because it was all on show. The sort o' square, and people! The better off lived down there on that corner. Their husbands worked in Edinburgh, and they were posh. And this side, was my stepmother, eventually, with a gang of children. Nice children, they're still, and then we lived at the top of the square.

---

[1] It is sometimes said that the Dicksons were the last family to leave. However, they lived in a house which was some way from the main village.

One benefit of the fact that the Binn Village became popular with holidaymakers is that a large number of postcards of the village were published. These give us a good idea of how it looked in the days when it was still a thriving community.

Above - a postcard of the High Binn, conveying something of the spectacular view which the inhabitants enjoyed. Alan Barker collection.
Below- this postcard shows the road from Kinghorn Loch on the left, and the Low Binn adjacent to it. Alan Barker collection.

So you could see all that was going on, that side and that side, and in the centre were two, maybe you still see them, taps for getting the water through and a pail.

You had two pails ..... there was nothing inside, and then you had to come out the house, and go along and round the other end to get to the toilet. Aye, it was a block, aye. ..... I was pretty agile when I was young, I went out the back window. Just leap out the back. So I could, sort of, allow a bit time. Leap out the bedroom window, and up a wee hill. We'd no gardens.

Oh, there was [a building] called the auld school. It was a school when the Binn Village was a proper place, and miners' children went to this, a very nice building. One great room. ..... we had to go to Burntisland to school, but [the auld] school now turned into the means of entertainment and they had dances all the time, especially on Saturday night. It was good; it was a great help. If anybody had a party, they could have it in the auld school. And aye, my sister and I were allowed to go to the dances, 'cause my dad was there, hopping merrily. Old set dances, and waltzes and the steps were up in this school for the desks, but they were taken out, and all the gossipy women sat along the wall on this, and watched who was dancing with who, and, oh what a set up. My dad always loved dancing. ..... and he was a very handsome man, you know. .....

[The music was provided by a] melodeon. ..... Aye, like an accordion. I thought, call it a *melodeon*! And if it was a special time, the melodeon came from Kirkcaldy; he was awfully good. Aw, he just brought the thing to life. He just sat up on this step, and played away for hours. And then there was a room, about that width, but long; that had been the school and they danced there.

[There was food] if it was a special, somebody's birthday, or something like that. No, the drink was taken down at the Binn, before they came! It was just beer men drank. Aye, there was no trouble. I suppose they just had a drink to stand for the limitations of everything. ..... oh, it was good, and we were allowed to go, my sister and I. ...... And we would go tae about, maybe about twelve, and then we just kept on when we grew up. But we were always allowed to go, yeah. ..... people behaved themselves. I think they did anyway!

Oh, [the auld school] was used for every social occasion ....., it had a marvellous floor, set wood. And it had been the school when it was the mining village of the district. And it was looked after and it was kept clean. And the raised platform that had been the school desks was where folk that didnae dance sat. ..... that was quite good fun.

..... they would have special things, ... I don't think poetry was read or anything like that. There was lots o' singing done and somebody would come with a violin ..... But they were Scottish songs .....

It was a den of iniquity! It was a damn good way for young people to have a life because, when you went up the hill, there was walls built, and you went through the opening in the wall, ... the hill side kept out flat for quite a bit on the *down* side o' the wall. And everybody just sat on that wall or if you felt like a dance you went over the wall and did it on the earth. ..... unless there had been a big quarrel or something, they all went there, a' the men. And we, we got warned, "Now, keep away from the Binn when the men are there," you know. Course the men didn't want us. But we used to listen in and get our education .....

So there was the shop and there was the Binn, the top o' the Binn was a 'place', there was nothing there except a wall. Everybody went there. And down in the Low Binn was the Sunday school and you went there on Sunday.

Aye, yes. I had Sunday school. My mother made [me go], my mother was a Christian woman, you know. My dad wasn't, he was from the Hielands! But we'd to go in if we felt like it ..... my mother would have preferred us to go. ..... the front row was the best row.

The best people lived there. Mainly they were from the Highlands and they were as tight as ....., didn't mix. I used to love their Highland accent. And then there was the football pitch; it's maybe still there. And that was called Princes Street; you'd a number and ..... that was the best.

They were respectable people who'd nothing to do with where we lived. ..... we didn't have our mother, you see, but these people had known her, before she had to go to the sanatorium, ... she was brought up in the Peebles-shire, in a farm and she was a very lady-like person, didn't have anything to do with these, so there was a lot of notice taken of, specially me, 'cause I used to chatter. But they were quite separate; you would hardly believe it. And then the next row was the working men ..... And then above that was another row of, maybe worked in Edinburgh or ..... would have some kind of a job. And then there was another row where the shop was. And ..... then there was the square, and it was quite a mixture of people. .....

..... all the boys played football. We were taught, latterly, to play hockey on it. The Binn was a good place. ..... adults were really in charge. You didn't get to do things that were gonna injure [you.] I think it was just the right size .....

..... quite a lot of Edinburgh people bought the houses, which were a room and a kitchen.

.....Aye, and the sea would be blue. "Oh, she's looking at the view!" you know. That was me, but I think that was a real, asset to my life. I appreciated that view as a child. And you could climb up this wall and I had two foot bits and I could just hang over the wall. And there it was, spread out. And just look down, down, down. But then, chalk from cheese from your upbringing, I'm sure.

..... we got to be caddies [at the Golf Club.] Oh, that was a terrible ..... my friend and I, she had been brought up in Leith, but when she came to live in the Binn we became very friendly, in the same class at school, and we were coming up one day, and we always went in the caddie hut it was called, for the caddies; just to carry on wi' the boys, and sort o' have a laugh. There wisnae any boys there, but two men came out to golf and they were 'nobs' from the back of Kilrie and that places, and we said, "There's no boys." "Where are they then? Where the hell are they? Where the bloody hell," [said the] gentlemen. "They've all gone home, there's a football." And one o' them said, "Come on then, you come," and we looked at them ..... "We'll give you one shilling and sixpence for nine holes." Oh, that was fine, get in the pictures for one and sixpence, so my friend and I ..... we caddied ever after. They just waited on us, coming out of school, and we got these one and sixpences, it was good.

..... And the caddying, oh, but the mothers, up in the Binn, they created hell; we were "taking the money away fae the laddies"! The laddies were too damn lazy to do it themselves ..... The men waited on us and we'd come, they well stewed from their lunch, and, "Come on, then. Just do nine." My friend [and I], we just blethered to ourselves, and handed the club. You knew what they needed; they couldnae play golf anyway. But they were all sort of, 'well-on', with a good lunch. .....

We came [to Burntisland], once a week, to Low's. ..... It was a cheap grocer's. And came once a week, and carted it all up, the bags ..... but the vans came up, all the time. The bread van came and the coal. Aye, fish came, not very often but they [came], it was lovely, good fish. And the butcher came, three times a week. They had to go up there to get custom.

..... I used to come home every weekend to clean the house. There was a saying, "Oh, Jean's hame," and I thought, "What the hell do they say that for?" "Oh, well, just look up the square and see the windows been cleaned." But that was the first thing I did. They *never* cleaned the windows, and you couldnae see out the damned things, if I wisnae hame every weekend.

Walter Carstairs recalls his holidays:

Now my earliest thing I can tell you about was we travelled back and forward [from Edinburgh] to Burntisland, as you know, every weekend. I wasn't even at the school. But my mother took me to Burntisland, and a pram, and up came my two sisters, and my father to the Golf Club, the clubhouse and she would be sitting there waiting on them coming up and then they would push her up the hill, which was a terrible trail to go to.

Top and middle - the High Binn from different viewpoints. In the middle picture, the shale bings can be seen. Bottom - the Low Binn. Alan Barker collection.

These two old postcards of the High Binn give a more detailed impression of the individual houses. Interestingly, the creator of the bottom one appears to have attempted to transform the original photograph into something more artistic!
Alan Barker collection.

We travelled on a Friday you understand. I used to get a line from my mother to allow bearer to leave school at so and so, three o'clock or something. And I used to run down what they call Wheel Brae, that was from near Newhaven, the Wheel Brae, and then along came this four-in-hand coach and I used to get up to the top beside the driver, ... that was to Granton and then over on the boat to Burntisland.

That [coach] was horse-drawn. 1912, I think was the first electric tramcar in Edinburgh. Every Friday afternoon, after I got this line to allow me to run down to the Wheel Brae, we call it, and I would get onto this four horses, up beside the driver, just from there to Granton ..... and in the boat, but I don't think we ever had a ticket. I don't think I ever had a ticket, all the time it ran.

Aye, and [at Burntisland] my mother used to push the pram and me in the pram. And she would shop and then carry on to the golf course. My father and my two sisters would arrive and then they would take the pram up the hill, and so on. Well it was our own house.

[We came across] every weekend. I've nae idea how many years we did that. ..... That was our summer holidays. My father, mother and my two sisters would travel. .....

The Pattons, I forget their names. That was all that came across as a group and they all had their own house. At that time it was [a high standard of living,] because we could afford to come to Burntisland and live.

..... you see if you were a wee bit 'toffee' you could hire auld Ecky Downie's prams, buses ..... In those days, they were all kind of coach things and they used to run from the station, right up to the High Binn, right by the Low Binn and up that road.

..... Novel freedom, novel freedom. And then they used to have concerts. There was a schoolhouse at one time. Aye, well there was concerts in there, Sunday, a free-for-all style. I can remember that, having to sing or recite or something like that. And then it was all dry closets[2] at the end of the houses. And you had your own closet, your own key.

Now there was a shop there. I think I can remember this shop. At the top, as ye come up the road that comes up and ye go in, there was a shop just about there and that was carried on for many a year, but, ye know, they werena class shops in these days.

I can remember going to ..... Picardy Place in Edinburgh, it was a hall, a big hall. My father was made Provost for the High Binn. Aye, and, oh, it was a great occasion and I wisna very big at that time, just a small boy. Well, there was a big meeting; I could remember that. There was a very, very big meeting; all the High Binners were there. See it was all, more or less, Edinburgh [folk] that lived up there.

..... It was all gone, the old works were gone, and the houses were good condition. And we stayed in Princes Street in the High Binn, and this big meeting was held, and everybody attended this big meeting and he was duly appointed Provost of the High Binn. I can always remember that, as clear as can be. That was more or less the thanks for the work he must have had done.

Ah, now the Low Binn was still there. A lot of Edinburgh people went and lived at the Low Binn. Well, well, not many, because there were only two rows of houses at the Low Binn, and well you used to see it from the golf course, you see. I remember, in the early days of the golf course, the Low Binnhouses ....., it was only the ruins then.

Coming on from there were the years that I was managing to go with them and to the school at the same time and I can remember quite clearly walking down from the High Binn, as you know there were no houses at all there, just country. When we came down Cromwell Road, I had to run and I could see the town clock from there, before the store built the Co-operative, in the lane there, I could see the town clock. And I'd be the one that would say, "Ten to eight." .....
Ad that was it, ten to eight, that was all right, ten minutes to get to the boat was no bother. And then that carried on every week. And mum would say, "You better run see the time." Course I

---

[2] As opposed to a flushing toilet.

ran, and it must have been Cromwell Road, and I saw. These big houses would be there at that time, and I would see the clock and yell what time it was.

Annie Christie:

Well, there was nearly all big families, most of them had big families at the Binn, and, I mean when I was there, it was a' just children. But there was a lot o' Edinburgh people came across as well, like at weekends and things like that. But most o' the folk in the Binn had, well my mother only had two, but the rest o' them had big families, and there was a' the Meades and the Girvans ..... There were quite a lot o' them ..... the Coopers ..... everybody had a bigger family, but they was only but an' bens for everybody, [a room and a kitchen.]

The well was in the street, just at our door where we lived. We had the well at our door, but everybody in the street had to use it. Just an iron thing that you turned the handle on. And the toilets were away, round the next street. They were in a row, like. You had just dry toilets that you'd to walk away round there for. And then they had a washing house away up on the hill, everybody knew the big boiler that you had to light the fire [for] and boil their clothes, and just a washing tub and a washing board. That was how they did their washing. And then there was the school at the Binn where we used to go up. They had dances there at night and what they called maidens, the farm folk used to come and there was dancing there at night.

[Our house had] a lot o' steps up. It would be maybe about seven or eight steps up, no railings or anything, just steps up. Just a door and then there was a wee lobby, you just went into your ..... kitchen, and then the bedroom went off the kitchen. And I don't think there was any fireplaces in the bedroom, I canna mind o' that at all, but there was one in the kitchen, just a range thing, an open fire. But there was no water or anything in the house. Two beds, bed recesses, two in each room. ..... [One family] had about thirteen [in the same size of house.] But they were quite happy, I mean, and they were a' healthy. Their father ..... used to go down to Fernie the grocer's round about closing time and he used to get big ham ends and the kids would come out eating them, just how, they'd got a' the fat and everything on them. But, mind, they were a' healthy children.

[The village had] one wee shop, just, but it was just a sort o' wee grocer's shop, sweeties and bread and rolls and things like that they sold.

..... there was one, two, three, four streets where I lived, and there was two streets up above that, a sort o' wee hill and you went up and there was two streets up there. And then there was what we called the 'big square', where there was quite a lot o' houses in a sort o' a square. And then [there was] the 'wee square', that was where the two big houses were. Where the Dicksons lived and the McGillvrays; they were big houses. In fact, the McGillvrays' was a double storied house. And Mrs Dickson's was a sort o' L-shaped ..... It was quite a big house as well, but they had big families as well.

..... And Mrs Dickson, she thought she was, she came from Edinburgh at one time, and I think she thought she was the Queen o' the Binn. She fancied hersel' a bit, and the McGillvrays, they were, there was quite a lot of the McGillvrays and they lived in Craigholm Crescent for a wee while, after they came from the Binn, the older McGillvrays.

..... Ah-ha, well there was rows [of toilets], aye, there was a whole row of them, and you'd to a' use your, your number was on them, your door, what your number o' your house was, and you used that. And then that Mr Kay, he was at ..... that big house down at where the aluminium, where Alcan was. Whinnyhall. He used to come up wi' a cart and a horse and empty a' the toilets once a week. They were in a big house doon at Whinnyhall ..... You just a' kept your own wee bit clean.

..... And the road down to where Whinnyhall was, was just rough cobble stones, it was, it was really hard on your feet when you were going down to the Sunday School, but we used to cut into the fields and go down through the grass. But I think Alcan sorted a' that road after that.

Mr Henderson from the Erskine Church ran the Sunday School, and we used to a' go down there on a Sunday afternoon. Rosie Muir, she played the wee organ thing, and there was two o' the elders used to come, a Mr Todd and a Mr Turnbull ..... then, of course, Mr Henderson wisnae well enough to walk up to the Binn, 'cause he was quite an old man, at least we thought he was quite old, but I think he really was quite an old man. So, when we went to Meadowfield, we still went up to the Binn Sunday School from Meadowfield, but he asked us if we would come to the Erskine Church because he couldnae, no longer could come up, walk up to the Low Binn. So that's when we started going to the Erskine Church.

..... there was no school at the Binn village when we were there. It was just what they called the school; it had been a school at one time, but no in our time. .....

Used to go up the woods and right up and round. We were called the 'Binnites'. The shipyard, the folk at the shipyard houses called us the 'Binnites'. ..... that's what we got called, "Oh, here's the Binnites coming."

Annie and her family moved to Meadowfield in Burntisland when she was ten years old.

Then when we first came to Meadowfield the houses were sort o' white emulsion, we got called 'Chinatown'. That was what they called us; they used to call this place 'Chinatown'. It wisna' Meadowfield, it was 'Chinatown'. ..... it was really wonderful, just, we couldnae believe it; hot water and toilets and everything, it was really great. ..... Aye, we really liked it. Well, a lot of [families moved at the same time.] A lot of the big families didn't come, like the Fishers and the Coopers and the Clissolds. They didnae come down till the two blocks were built on the Dollar Road there; they were four apartment houses, so they didn't come down till they were built. They were building them just after we came here. But there was still people in the Binn after they came down as well.

Jim Harvey:

..... next to me there, was a fruit shop wi' the Archers. Now, eventually, it was a Dan Todd that had it, and he was modern, he got a motor car and a lorry, and that was when I got away wi' him on a Saturday afternoon, his country round away up, and that took you up past the shale mine, the Binn Village, and he delivered his stuff up to the Binn Village at that time, the Low Binn as well. It's hard to realise that the Low Binn, there was a Low Binn, wi' so many houses there at one time. ..... there was more houses up the top, but as far as I can, I think there was two rows o' houses there, but there's been such a lot o' stuff come over, wi the aluminium, it's a' come forward to the road.

..... In these times, the Binn children got away early at night in the wintertime.

Jimmy Wilson:

I came to Burntisland when I was seven. ..... my dad got killed in the First World War. I think, at one time, my mother and sister and I had come here, or somewhere round about Fife for holidays, and she must have thought, at that time, this was a great place to bring up a family.

And that was why we came here. When we did come here, we stayed across where the gas works was, at that time. ..... In Thistle Street. We stayed there for two, three weeks till we got this house up in the Binn Village, and that's when we stayed there. We were there from 1922 until 1934.

This photo shows the horse drawn ice cream cart visiting the High Binn in the early 1930s, gaining access via the track from the east. The cart belonged to Luciani's of Kinghorn, and the ice cream vendor is George Murdoch.

Jimmy Wilson remembers most of the names, and the full line up from left to right (excluding the girls and the vendor) is: Tommy Montgomery, Charlie Patterson, Bert Murdoch, Alex Hood, Jimmy Wilson, Willie Cooper, David Blake, (unknown), Finlay Morrison, Willie Hartshorn, (unknown). Jimmy thinks that the girls were visitors from West Lothian.

Jimmy Wilson collection.

Well there was only two ways to get to the Binn Village. One was up the pathway from the clubhouse, and the other was away round, as you go now, to get up through, that's where the trucks, lorries, horses and carts, coal merchants and whatever, came to get to the village. You came right up through, and then, but when you got to the village it was all done in rows of houses. And the first row of houses went up in the front. There was quite a number of people stayed up the Binn, in the village at that time.

Well the High Binn and the Low Binn was two different places. There was only one person, that I ever mind of, who stayed in the Low Binn, and I'm sure that he worked, or he was a joiner wi' Tommy Henderson, who had that joiner's business where ..... Wilkie's building these houses now, in there. That was a joiner's shop and workshop, and he had, every Thursday he used to have furniture sales, second hand furniture, and he had them up above in that roof place.

..... When you went into [our] house [at the Binn Village], it was just a room and kitchen, but in the kitchen was two bed recesses. ..... when it was the summertime, I've seen twelve, fourteen in a bed!

..... But when you went through to the other room, there was only one bed; there was no recess but there was a bed. .....

Well, there wasn't any, like, modern conveniences like there is today, like sinks and wash hand basins in the house. All the water was outside in the well and you had to cart it in in a bucket. The toilets were dry ..... Charlie Kay was one o' the men who used to come and empty

94

the buckets and that, into a cart.

[We carried water] into the house in a bucket. Well, if you, in these days, ... wanted a bath, or when anybody in the house, or anybody wanted a bath, you waited till your parents were washing, doing the washing. Then after they finished the washing, you put a blanket up on the washhouse window, filled up the boiler, heated the water and had a bath in one o' the wooden tubs.

..... there was a 'washing house', but I mean, there wasnae any washing machines, it was a' scrubbing boards and scrubbing brushes.

[The adults] could do the same if they wanted it, and that's what they did. They had their bath in the washhouse, they just went in and locked the door and bailed the water out the boiler into the tub. [The water was heated] by a boiler, in the corner. Coal fired; it was a coal-fired boiler.

..... they had it worked out that they got plenty time to do their washing. I mean if it was a good day, you could get three or four people in on the one day in the wash house, because there were drying greens, a drying green.

..... every area in the village had a washhouse. I mean [ours] was in the square. When you went further down there was always a washhouse where you could get in. [The number of families which used our washhouse was] maybe a couple o' dozen.

[Toilets were] all outside, it was a row of buildings, just, individually, a toilet, dry toilet.

Jimmy Wilson is in the centre of this photograph,
taken at the Binn Village. On the left of the photo is
Willie Cooper, and on the right, Johnny Hood.
At the back is Jimmy's sister, Ivy.
Jimmy Wilson collection.

..... there was a shop. I don't remember the shop as it was. There was always a shop there, but I understand that when the mines were working properly, it was run by the Co-operative from here, and there was a Burntisland lady used to work in it; Agnes Leslie worked in that shop up the Binn and she, eventually, she finished up in the Co-operative in the High Street, in the office.

..... there was a football pitch there, and they had dances and there was a part of the school, which was never destroyed, and it had a lovely floor and they used to have dances in there. The school [had] closed, I think around about 1905, when the mine closed, and the miners began to shift from here to the Lothians where the mines were still working. [The old school became] sort o' a community centre. They used to have dances in there and, I think, once or twice, I think there was Burns Suppers in there. ..... the WRI that was started in the Low Binn, ... that was started by some of the women up in the village, in the Binn Village.

..... I used to, at 12, mind, 12 and 13 years of age, I was carrying hundredweight bags of coal, up in the Binn Village. And ..... I've walked round that golf course four times in one day, carrying clubs. Well, 12, up tae I left school. I did have a strong back, but it's a bit weaker now!

This picture of the High Binn was taken in 1953. Most of the houses have had their roofs removed. This would have accelerated their deterioration, but - probably of more importance to the owners - it would have saved them money, as in those days no rates were payable on roofless properties. In the following year, 1954, the last residents left the village.
Iain Sommerville collection.

Chapter 5

The Shipyard

An aerial view of Burntisland shipyard. Iain Sommerville collection.

The Burntisland Shipbuilding Co Ltd was founded in 1918 by Amos and Wilfred Ayre. In its lifetime of just over 50 years, the company built approximately 310 ships.

The shipyard closed in 1969, after a long and chequered history. The 1960s were difficult times for Scotland's long established shipyards, but the yard at Burntisland was, on the face of it, doing reasonably well. However, problems over one contract were to come to a head in 1968, and were to prove insurmountable.

The ship in question was the 'Ohrmazd', a fast cargo liner for the East & West Steamship Company of Karachi, Pakistan. This ship was effectively being paid for by the British Government, as part of its foreign aid to Pakistan. But its construction was plagued by wrangles over the specifications and contract terms between the shipyard and the shipowners. These led to serious delays in completing the ship. The delays in turn led to the incurring of punitive financial penalties by the shipyard, with which it was simply unable to cope.

The ship was completed in November 1968, but the damage had been done. Burntisland Shipyard went into liquidation the following month. Two other ships were completed after the 'Ohrmazd', and the yard closed on 19 July 1969, just over 51 years after the keel of the first ship, the 'Sunbank', was laid on 25 June 1918.

Another aerial view of Burntisland Shipyard.
BHT collection.

Shipyard Employees' Discussion Group

Ian McLeod, himself at one time a welder at Burntisland Shipyard, chaired two informal discussion sessions with former employees:

> Tom Allan *(Welder; latterly Quality Control Inspector)*
> Alex Ferguson *(Welder)*
> Tom Lawrence *(Welder)*
> Bob Miller *(Contracts Manager)*
> Bill Strawn *(Loftsman)*
> Johnston Wood *(Manager)*

Tom Allan, Alex Ferguson and Tom Lawrence attended both sessions, and Bob Miller, Bill Strawn and Johnston Wood attended only the second one.

The following extracts from the transcripts of the discussions give an evocative, and at times hilarious, picture of working life in the shipyard.

Personal Introductions

Tom Allan:

I was an electric welder ....., and to get on wi' management, I felt I got on very well wi' management, because I was the type o' boy that wisnae one that wanted to argue all the time about jobs or that and if I was told to do a thing, well I tried to do it the right way and the way I had been shown by the journeymen who had taught me. One was a John Wilson fae Cowdenbeath, a very hotheaded man, but a very good man to learn your trade with. And if you didnae do what you were told, you got a kick on the backside, but other than that he was very good to learn you your trade.

And I got on very well wi' him and very well wi' the management and through time, I became a charge hand mysel' in the welding department. And then ..... the quality control department came in, and I was a quality control inspector for quite a few years, until I gave it up and went ..... to be a postman because I was sick wi' the amount o' strikes and things that was in the shipyard at that time.

Alex Ferguson:

..... I started in the yard in 1947, October about the 13th I think it was, I started my apprenticeship. It was actually the brother-in-law that got me interested in it, Mr Paton, and I went doon and I seen ..... Dod Rae [who] was the foreman at the time, and I went round and I walked into the office and he sat and looked at me and he said, "Do you think you'd like to be a welder?" ..... I didnae actually hae a clue what it was, but I says, "Aye," and I started on the following Monday, as an apprentice welder. The first boy I got sent wi' was Billy Roy, which was a local fella his sel'.

..... and then they brought in what they cried a Fusarc machine, which was a thing that weighed aboot a hundredweight and a half. And it was a pretty big machine, heavy. So Billy and I went on it, and I was at the back, what they cry chipping the slag off, it left a brown slag at the back. And you got a hammer and chisel and you had to chip this off before you could put a newer run on the top. And I worked wi' that, and went hame wi' a lot o' sore eyes at night, because there was nae shields round it to break the glare. And one night I was sitting and the water was streaming doon my eyes, and, oh, teabags and a'thing, putting on to try and cool them

99

doon and the old man said, he says, "If it's that bad, pack it in." But I persevered and you got applied to it, sat wi' your back to the machine and a' that. .....

I enjoyed it, I enjoyed my time in the shipyard, because they were a' good lads. A lot o' local fellas. ..... I landed doon there in a good time, because it was just after the war and they couldnae get the berths emptied quick enough to get another ship on to it. And it was good; overtime was there, you could dae this and we used to go on the Friday night, where you worked the Friday, went hame, got your tea, came back, you worked the Friday night round to Saturday morning. And it was there for you; you only had to get doon and dae it, that was it. I really enjoyed it, ye ken? But it just sort o' started drying up a wee bit after that. They seemed to hit a big peak for a guid two or three year, and then the shipyard started trying to get orders. And I got paid off once and I went up to the Grangemouth shipyard and worked up there for a wee while and when it picked up again, I got back in doon there again, and it was just sort o' oot and in. But that was actually the good years we got doon there, just right after the War. Really shouting for ships.

Tom Lawrence:

I was originally a Kinghorn man, where a' the good tradesmen came from! I started in the yard in ..... 1938. When I first went in for a job, I met Jimmy Smith, who was also a Kinghorn man. He asked who I was. I said, "Tom Lawrence from Kinghorn." He says, "Lawrence fae the 'horn, start the morn," so I had to report, it wis funny. Jimmy was a portly type o' man, wi' the navy blue suit, bowler hat, the old type, just much the same as Darkie Simpson was, the carpenter foreman, and big walrus moustache.

So I reported to the general store on the Monday morning and my job was giving out candles. It was all candles at that time. The main holds in the ships were lit by electricity wi' big clusters, but mainly, in double bottoms[1] and everything, it was all done wi' candles; hand caulking[2] and all that sort o' thing. And every bolt and nut and washer was all weighed; it all had to be given a line for the engineers, and this had to be weighed and given out. I suppose this was all statistics for the weight o' the ship and all the rest of it, for the launching.

So I was in there for about four or five month and then I was started as an apprentice welder by Dod Rae, who, by the way, I've got respect for him. I reckon he was a good foreman, fair and that was it. So, from there I had several apprentices in my time and then I mated up with, at the back end o' the yard thing, Tom Allan and I mated up. We usually worked in pairs because we found that when you were shifting gear, you were handling maybe three hundred feet o' cable, copper cable, and it was easier for two to handle these than one, especially if you were taking cables up the side o' a ship and so forth. So most of the welders, I would say them all, had a mate that worked on the piecework[3] system and split the tally between them. .....

..... And once we started moving onto the ships, we met very severe resistance from the riveters, because I think that they saw that it was the thin end of the wedge. We got complaints about the flashing light, so we got screens put up. We would leave our job for lunch, go back after the break and we'd find our screens were a' smashed up and this sort o' thing. And then the older men would turn round and say, "This is only a flash in the pan, laddie. You'll have a hammer in your hand before you're finished." So then the War came in and things started really

---

[1] Tom Lawrence explains the term 'double bottom': "The double bottom in a ship is, you've got the bottom, then you've got a tank top, where the cargo sits, and in between that is about three feet. They used it as ballast tanks, so that if the ship's empty, they can take her down in the water a bit to make her more stable in bad weather."
[2] Pressing material into joints to render them watertight.
[3] Iain McLeod explains: "We worked piecework, i.e. paid by the piece. For welders the piece was one foot of weld. There were four weld descriptions: flat, horizontal, vertical and overhead. Flat had the lowest rate."

moving, because I can always remember, the first big job we had was the deck on a ship that had all the butts welded, and it was a' just the seams o' the deck that were riveted.

Bob Miller:

Now my start date in the Burntisland Shipbuilding Company was in 1944 where it was the menial tasks of carrying plans to the apartments in the yard from the drawing office. My intention, which followed, was to become an apprentice in the drawing office. The journeying through the yard would familiarise me with all the departments. I was with the Burntisland Shipbuilding Company until it closed down in the liquidation and, at that time, I was in the position of Contracts Manager.

..... Once established in the drawing office, you received a full five-year apprenticeship in those days and you picked up an awful lot in that period, from the workmen, or the other draughtsmen of various ages, during your working period. After the five years concluded, you were then classified as a journeyman draughtsman. Shortly after that I moved up and soon became Chief Draughtsman in the drawing office, so one can assume that by that time I knew all of its inner workings.

Bill Strawn:

I started in the shipyard in 1943, August '43, fourteen year old. I was a wee, young laddie. I was following my brother into the shipyard, Andrew, he was an apprentice shipwright at the time, and I first started with Ben Broxburgh. He was the foreman riveter. From then I spent two years 'catch boy' and 'heater boy'. In 1945 I started my apprenticeship with the shipwrights. I was wi' the shipwrights for the five year. I was two year on the tools, outside the yard, and then I went into the loft[4], and that's where I stayed, in the loft.

..... I think the easiest way to explain loft work is the transition from the drawing side of the ship, and all the bits and pieces and making it into the full size templates that had to go out to the platers, ... mainly the platers. For example, we had to support, give the information for all the frames on the ship, all brackets for the ship, had to develop all the shell plates for the ship, and, well, basically everything that was needed for any ship that was developed in the loft and passed out.

I got on ..... great with the [management side], because when I first started it was Willie Graham, I think it was, that was the foreman loftsman at the time, and another good chappie was Geordie Johnson, he come from Leith. ..... I think they took me under their wing. .....

And I used to go to night school, to Edinburgh, twice a week. We used to get away from the shipyard at half past three in the afternoon, catch the train at four o'clock, five o'clock, go to Edinburgh, do my ..... night school and get back into Rosyth again about ten o'clock at night. That was two nights a week for aboot three year. But it paid dividends for me, because ..... I entered an exam for the Worshipful Company of Shipwrights. It was an annual exam and in 1948, I was second in Britain. I was first in Scotland .....

..... When I first started in the shipyard I went in as a 'catch boy', and my memories of the first day when I went there was that Ben Broxburgh sent me round to what they called the market. Now, the market was in the first shed and it was where, first thing in the morning, all the riveters and the 'heater boys' ..... and the 'catch boys' all congregated and they were dispersed to where they were going and who was going wi' who, as regards 'catch boys' and the riveters, and the 'heater boys'.

---

[4] Ian McLeod explains: "The loft was a vast room, where the loftsmen used the drawings to create wooden templates of parts of the ship. These templates, which were actual size, were used in the manufacture of the parts. The loft was also the quietest place in the shipyard!"

On this page and the opposite page are four photographs of work in progress at the shipyard. Unfortunately, there is very little detailed information available about the photos. The bottom one on the opposite page was taken in 1943. The top one on this page was taken at a launch, at the moment the ship enters the water. Ian McLeod recalled that the actual launch of a ship was a time of great nervousness for everyone involved.

BHT collection.

So I got put with a family that come from Rosyth, the Douglases, now they were a famous family at that time; the father and they had four, I think they had four, brothers, working in the yard. And they collared me and they took me, and I think the ship that was, the first ship I went onto was the 'Empire Mackendrick', if that was the second of the aircraft carriers getting built, and they took us down, they were doing about the third stern, or something, and it was down into the bowels o' the ship. And I was absolutely petrified, if I can mind right, because 1943 and there was still the possibilities o' German planes coming over the Forth and I'm saying, how in the name o' goodness am I going to get oot o' here if the Germans come. But I carried on.

The 'catch boys', once again ..... the 'heater boys' used to throw the red hot rivets up and you had to catch them and stick them in the hole for the 'hauder on' to do, to put it in, and woe betide you if you didn't get them in quick enough. I worked there as a 'catch boy' for, it was, I think, about a year, and then I was promoted, if you can say that, to a 'heater boy' and you got a wee bit more money then, because at the end o' the week, it all depended if you were a good 'heater boy' and the riveters put in so many rivets and they got paid piecework, you got what they called a 'bung'. You got a couple o' pound extra at the end of the week as a 'bung'. So that lasted until 1945 when I left the riveting department and I started with Mr Darkie Simpson as an apprentice shipwright. So that was my riveting days.

..... if you burnt the rivet, they were like ..... clinker at the end o' that, clinker at the end o' a rivet. Your rivet had to be nice and yellow for to go in the hole right.

..... there was two 'hauder ons'. They had the machine 'hauder on' and the hammer 'hauder on', and if you were daein' a deck and they used to fling the rivets up to you, you'd to scamper across the scaffolding from the deck, haud them up for him 'cause he had what they called a long shaft, a long shafted hammer, and woe betide you if you dropped them. And mind, in they days, a fourteen year old laddie up, I would say, maybe about twenty feet up in the air, running on nia inch planks, running across and stick this and that there. When you think o' health and safety in they days!

Johnston Wood:

..... I was the Shipyard Manager.

..... my memories go back before I was employed in the shipyard, when I was a school boy, way back pre-war. And one o' the things that stands out in my mind is the shipyard buses at teatime. For a small boy playing on the Links it was some sight to see seven, eight or nine double-decker buses roaring along the High Street, along the Kinghorn Road, bearing in mind there were no traffic lights, no traffic islands, there were no parked cars, there were very few private cars, it was usually horses and carts. So they had the clear road and it was almost, well, like the Monte Carlo Rally when they came charging up, and no one dared cross the road, the High Street or that. But it was a daily occurrence and it only happened at teatime and was finished by ten minutes, and then everything reverted back to the sleepy old village.

The other thing that I do remember, in the morning when you first wakened up, you knew which way the wind was blowing because you could hear the rivet hammers louder or not so loud with the east or west wind. The other thing that sticks in my mind was, coming out the school, on Cromwell Road, and seeing the big boilers coming from David Rowen ..... on their low loaders being transported down the Toll and down Cromwell Road and it was an impressive sight. They had no police escort, in those days; it wasn't required. And to let you know the size of them, sometimes they could not get under the railway viaduct at the bottom o' the street, and they had to be rolled off and skidded through and then rolled back on the low loaders.

So, that's the main things I remember, but when I left school, I do remember my first interview was with Mr Hall, the Chief Draughtsman, and he was very particular about where I had been and what I had been doing. Very explicit on what I was going to be doing and what was expected of me, which was really compulsory night school.

Well, when I started on the first day, it was quite traumatic, the hustle and bustle o' the drawing office, coming straight from a quiet classroom to this business activity. And of course, you were doing office boy's duties and it was quite, what should I say, quite stressful when you were expected to know all the vocabulary and terminology, all the geography of the shipyard. But as we know, you're not expected to learn that all in the one day.

So after a few weeks, you were allowed on the drawing board, and you started again, at the bottom of the heap, and you started to progress, mainly with the help and experience of the other senior apprentices and the journeymen, until you finished your apprenticeship. In the meantime, you had been going thre nights a week to night school to get your certificate. .....

Then, after my apprenticeship, Mr John Wright, the shipyard manager, promoted me to the outside management team. Again, you were the bottom o' the heap, the junior to the assistant to the dock manager. The terms o' reference for the management were always the same, you had to learn the vocabulary and the geography o' the place. You had to liaison with all the trades and the departments. You had the supervision of all the surveys for Lloyds and the owners. You had the quality control with the subcontractors, to see that we fulfilled our contracts. Then you were really in charge, at your own level, of the production, planning and control.

And it was noticed, after I left the dock and was in the plating sheds, that you had the three basic methods of production. You had the flow production, batch production and the unit production. The flow production, as everyone knows, would be the frame setting and then the shell plates. The batch production would be the double bottom units, and the unit would be deckhouses and the funnels. Now all these had to be integrated between the loft, the plater, the welder. We had the joiner, the blacksmith, the engineer. You had the plumber, the electrician and the painter. Then we had the riveters, we had caulkers, we had the stagers, the temporary light men, the crane men and slingers, the iron stores, the security, the safety men, all these had to be integrated, and I can say that most o' the men in the yard were their own managers. They did their own production planning and they did their own control. They were given their jobs and they did their own supervision and everything just went very well indeed.

Ian McLeod:

..... 'boy labourers', well, when I started in the yard at fifteen, that's what I was. I was a 'boy labourer', and I worked in number four shed to start with and then here, there and everywhere. I ended up in the stores for a while and when I was sixteen, that's when the apprenticeship started.

The Workforce and Working Relations

Tom Allan:

Well, the men, they come from a' round Fife, mainly Cowdenbeath, Kelty, Lochgelly, Rosyth, Kirkcaldy, Kinghorn, they were a' round Fife and they used to travel, at first, when I stayed, before I was working age, they came on bikes. They used to travel up and down from Cowdenbeath, and that wi' their bikes. And then the buses come into force and the wages was a wee bit better, and the men seemed to manage to get a bus fare, instead o' pushing the bikes up and down the Cowdenbeath Road. And they were a great lot o' men to work wi', and very friendly. You had a lot o' good laughs and fun. And I thoroughly enjoyed it, and ..... we had a busy time after the War. I think there was one year we built thirteen boats in the one year. Which was quite a bit o' doing. Some were small ones like small oil carriers, I think they were at that time. I think we made four in the one berth, if I mind right; they were small enough for that.

The 'Discoverer', pictured after her launch on 30 August 1954; delivered to the Pan Ore Steamship Company in April 1955. BHT collection.

The 'Shaftesbury', built for the Alexander Shipping Company and launched on 5 April 1958. BHT collection.

The 'Beaverpine' shortly after her launch on 18 June 1962. She was built for Canadian Pacific Steamships Ltd. BHT collection.

Aye, and we had the two aircraft carriers, was it two or three aircraft carriers we built? Aircraft carrier plus carrying grain; they were grain carriers, but there were a flight deck on them and that, for to help out during the War. And we built frigates as well, for the Navy during the War. So we really had a busy time. .....

Tom Lawrence:

..... At the same time there was camaraderie in the yard. It was the shipyard; it was a great place to work. So, later on, when the war came in, they brought in women to tack up[5], and I was asked to take on the welding school to teach them vertical and overhead. And these girls did a good job. They were on the double bottoms wi' the carpenters and tacking up a' the sections and everything, to save a welder's, a competent welder's time doing this, so that the welders came in at the back o' these people and finished the job off. These women did quite a bit o' work on the aircraft carriers on the upper deck, the flight deck; two or three o' them up there. And ..... I never had so many cakes in my life, at that time! And we were tested with Canadians who were coming in. The minesweepers, at that time, were old wooden trawlers, and they were manned by Canadians. And they used to have their eyes on the girls, of course, and I had to lock the door and keep everything out. But this went on for quite a while, and then I went back to the tools .....

~ ~ ~ ~ ~

Alex Ferguson: ..... they a', everybody seemed to get on thegither, ye ken? And everybody kent everybody else and chitchat and just banter back and forrit. You had sign languages tae in the shipyard .....

Tom Allan: Same when the managers were on site, the round hat, you put your hand up and made it like a round hat and you kent the managers was aboard. There was a lot o' sign language 'cause the noise was really so bad, you couldnae talk to one another. You maybe had two or three rivet squads, and caulkers and you were trying to talk, it was impossible, so you needed sign language.

Disputes and Demarcation

Tom Lawrence: ..... some of the young journeymen were brought in to the welding department, and they were brought in on a sort of temporary card, which caused a bit o' friction, because once they became competent they felt that they were in the same union, the Boilermakers' Union, you see? So we managed to get them, eventually, brought in to a full card, so that made everything equal. That made it a lot easier. .....

~ ~ ~ ~ ~

Tom Lawrence: We went on strike for thirteen weeks to get extracting fans for the double bottom. Eventually we got them and they put one pushing in at one end, and one drawing out at the other. .....

~ ~ ~ ~ ~

Alex Ferguson: ..... everybody in the shipyard, at that time, every trade had their thing to dae and you didnae encroach on theirs. Then within the yard, they brought in what they cried flexibility, where I could go and help a plater or a plater could help a welder within the Boilermakers' Society, but you couldnae go o'er and take a hammer and start knocking wi' the carpenters. But there was a bit come in there, where they were that short o' welders that they started letting the carpenters and the platers tack up their own work.

---

[5] Ian McLeod explains the term 'tack': "A tack is a preliminary strip of metal welded in place to join two parts, prior to the final welding."

Tom Lawrence: They took me into the wee shed, to take over the carpenters so they could tack up. The carpenters, to understand, they assembled everything, and coming away from the riveting, to the welding, you found out that a lot o' the stuff, instead o' being bolted up, was tacked. So I taught the carpenters to do vertical and overhead. I had about, oh, twenty machines along one side o' the wee shed, next to the berths, and they a' did about a fortnight or three weeks, and they a' passed out, which made a big difference. 'Cause it suited the welders, we hated tacking up, it was a waste o' time as far as we were concerned.

Alex Ferguson: But that, that caused a bit o' friction tae, Tam, because some o' them started getting a wee bit mair gallus and it wisnae three inch tack they pit in, they were wanting to dae a foot o' welding, and then you were coming up and looking at it and saying to yersel', "Who's been on the job before me?" It was the carpenters wanting to dae mair than what they shoulda been daein'. And that caused a bit o' friction tae. Because everybody in they days, tried to look after their ain job. There was always that fear at getting paid off, that somebody else could dae your job. .....

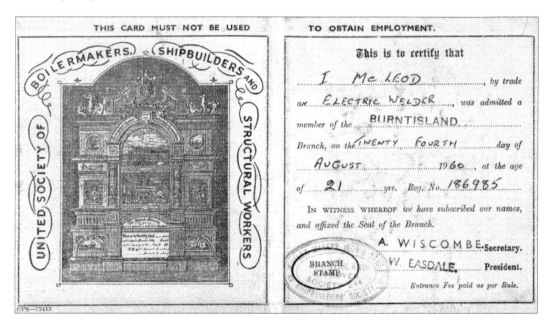

Above - Ian McLeod's union card. Right - the late Alex Mackinnon's union card.

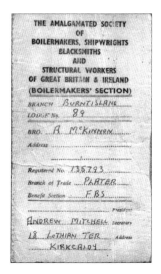

Tom Lawrence: ..... This was the same, this was the same wi' the blacksmiths. The blacksmiths used to do a lot o' hammer work, the big heavy stuff, and when the wire machines come in, they used to do a bit o' welding, fire welding, in the fire. But when the machines come in they realised that they could cut a lot o' their work out by using the machines. So there was a bit o' argument went on for a while and then they realised that, well, they're doing their own work, why no' let them do it. So I was put in to the blacksmiths' shop for aboot three month with ..... Ernie Petrie, the blacksmith, and he and big Ginger, I don't know what Ginger's name was, he come fae Cowdenbeath or someplace, but they had two machines in there, eventually, which they were able to do things like the bolsters for where the anchor pockets went down, and the hosepipes, and that sort o' thing. And, eh, they were a' fabricated after that, by them.

Alex Ferguson: Course the plumbers come there, an' a', Tam, and they started grabbing wee bits o' work fae welding and a' the rest o' it. And the plumbers had welders tae.

Sir Wilfred Ayre

Sir Wilfred Ayre at his desk. BHT collection.

Bob Miller: ..... Sir Wilfred Ayre was a very clever and forthright Tynesider who had come up from the Tyne, prior to 1917 with his brother, Amos, to set up what became the Burntisland Shipbuilding Company. So they had to find the site and then view the possibilities it had and dimensions of ships and so on. They were obviously exceptionally clever naval architects and Amos, the brother of Sir Wilfred, he became a Sir Amos prior to the honour being bestowed upon Wilfred. And the brother, Amos, who was slightly the elder, worked with the Government directly on seafaring and shipbuilding matters, down in London. And Sir Wilfred was the brother who controlled the operations and the obtaining of orders for ships, which they had done. ..... He would come up to the drawing office and stand up over your plan and you weren't supposed to stand and then fold your arms, you were to carry on working on it, and that was quite a, you were, got enjoyment out of it, insofar as he had deigned to come up and look at you trying to complete this drawing. But he was always very pleasant, in that regard. He gave you complimentary remarks on it. He wouldn't pull you down as it were, but latterly, of course, he retired from shipbuilding and the company was then taken over by Rea Brothers of London who were the owners ultimately.

Johnston Wood: ..... As duties o' the office boy, you had to fetch and carry plans, you had to answer the telephone; there was only one telephone in the office. And this was the day I told Sir Wilfred that Mr Hall was too busy to see him! The phone went, I answered the phone, and I should have said, "Who's speaking?" but the gruff voice said, "Mr Hall?" and I looked and Mr Hall was in a committee meeting with the owner and Lloyds etc, and of course, Mr Hall was like God. An office boy wasnae gonna go in and interrupt that meeting. So I said, I'm sorry, Mr Hall is too busy to come to the phone." Well there was an explosion on the end o' the phone! "My God! What is this? Who are you?" And I said, "Well, I'm sorry, he's in a meeting." "Oh, all right. Send him down to Sir Wilfred's room when he's free." Well the deed was done, so I barged into the meeting, told Mr Hall that Sir Wilfred wants him. The meeting broke up instantaneously; Mr Hall was away. .....

Tom Lawrence: ..... I was an apprentice, we used to have the welding holders burning out due to pressure o' work. Take note, Johnston, pressure o' work! And we used to go to the electricians' shop, at that time it was demarcation to get this ..... put in, which we used to do ourselves on the ship in a corner someplace, but anyway we used to get these things fixed up. So, I was standing in the electricians' shop wi' ma holder, which was on about ten feet o' cable and it was being attended to, and Wilfred barges in, "What the hell are you doing here?" "See," I said, "I'm wanting a holder fitted." My main impression was a bully, he was suffering fae high blood pressure and he needed a kick up the backside! Now, here was I wanting a holder fixed, if he had had any common savvy at all, he woulda' had spare holders already made up, ready for me to lift, 'cause it was costing me money to stand and wait on this thing getting fixed, but this is his attitude. I think he was a bully. I had no respect for that man whatsoever. .....

Tom Allan: The only meeting I had wi' Sir Wilfred, was myself and, I can't mind who it was, but we were sitting down the Green Isle[6] playing at noughts and crosses when a big man come over and said, "Who's winning?" and when I looked up, it was Sir Wilfred Ayre, and I dinna ken if I said he was winning or I was winning, but we got out the road as quick as we could!

Bill Strawn: I thought you were gonna say the classic, there, "Who's tea's that? Is it Lipton's?"

Tea Breaks

Tom Lawrence: Getting back to the early days, when we, when I first went in, anyway, that would be 1940. Purely riveting, the whole ships were held together wi' bolts. It was like one o' these wee Meccano sets, and when it rained, it dripped for hours afterwards. And in the wintertime it was horrific. Freezing, you were on slippery steel decks or whatever, and the most satisfying thing was the mealtime when you got up into the shed and somebody had a big steel plate and you used to put your bread and cheese out on a plank, the whole lot and they would go right along wi' this red hot plate and instant melted cheese. .....

~ ~ ~ ~ ~

Alex Ferguson: The queer thing aboot that wi' the drums o' tea wis, I aye used to wonder how the boys, some o' them could drink the tea that hot, and they fund oot it was the boys wi' the false teeth that could drink their tea hotter and they got mair oot the drum. I aye mind that, that was a laugh. I was sitting one day at the piece time and the boy says, turned roond to me and says, "That tea's red hot, how do you manage to drink it?" and the boy had false teeth so he

---

[6] The area covered by the shipyard included the Green Island, after which Burntisland is reputedly named.

The Prince of Wales (with bowler hat, stooping) visits Burntisland Shipyard in the mid 1930s. On the left of the picture, with his back to the camera, is Alex Mackinnon's uncle, Neilly McLennan. Slightly left of centre in the picture, attending to the machine, is John Mackinnon, father of Alex. Collection of the late Alex Mackinnon.

musta' been able to get that wee bit hotter tea into the mooth and got mair oot the drum than the other boy.

Tom Lawrence: This brings to my mind another complaint the men had, and the management didn't seem to see it. The break in the morning, usually had a break aboot nine o'clock and they made an official break o' ten minutes. And there was a little van there that sold tea and whasinames, and the men complained. They didnae get time to drink the tea, it was so hot. And it took the firm ages before they could realise that tell the man to put some cold water in it, or something to make it drinkable. I mean you've only ten minutes, you've got something here you canny even hold, it's that hot.

Alex Ferguson: But that was the time, Tom, when they tried to cut doon the tea break a bit. Because you were aye running aboot wi' a syrup tin wi' water in it trying to look for a fire to bile it, ye ken. Then it come roond, they had the idea o' putting on coffee and tea machines. And the only thing wi' that wis, the queue was that big, that it actually lasted longer than what it [did] for you to bile up the drum! So that ..... wisnae a success.

The Characters

Alex Ferguson: Well, there was Wullie Blake. He used to draw Mickey Mouse and that on the bulkheads, eh? He was a burner/caulker, Wullie Blake.

Tom Allan: I canny mind o' him at a'.

Alex Ferguson: Aye, he used to draw Mickey Mouse. He could just get a bit chalk and Mickey Mouse was on the bulkhead, ye ken? He was good.

~ ~ ~ ~ ~

Bill Strawn: The famous one I knew ..... was [Freddie] Muir. He was, to me, he was a legend, because there's still stories up in the golf park yet aboot [him]. ..... one o' the stories that still gets related was that, during the First World War, he used to say that he was getting chased by all these Germans, and he shot them all, but when they went to collect all their belongings on them, they all had this wee slip of paper in German. And he said, "I couldnae understand what it was," so he got it deciphered and what it said was, "Get Freddie Muir, dead or alive!" and that story still goes around.

~ ~~ ~ ~

Tom Allan: The only one that I ..... can mind aboot was auld Eck Scotland, he used to work in the furnace, but he was a great boy for getting the young chaps all together and telling them stories, and he used to jump backwards the width o' the railway from one rail to the other, and he used to have them trying this at dinner time and that, I can mind o' that. And he was quite a joker, this auld Mr Scotland.

~ ~ ~ ~ ~

Tom Lawrence: Old John Roxburgh, he was a boilermaker and he did a lot of fancy work such as boss plates and all that sort of thing. That's where the shaft comes out the ship, you have a sort of half round shape plate that's rolled and, like a tube, and clapped on each side. And he used to smoke thick black, and every time he smoked it, he used to blow it in your face! Aye, he was quite a character, quite a sense o' humour too, he had.

~ ~ ~ ~ ~

Tom Lawrence: I've got another poem by another old character, Sid Gibson, carpenter. He used to wear clogs in the wintertime. He was very political and this man lived in Mary Somerville's house. And he maintained that you saw a ghost. It's laughable at the time, but he got a new house through it, he got re-housed!

~ ~ ~ ~ ~

Johnston Wood: ..... Wi' Andrew Nichol and Davie Hay, the foremen shipwrights, I had a very pleasant afternoon siting the keel, which we had done in night school, but it was very, very informative when it was actually done on the practical side. And the same again was Mr David Mackie. he was the dockside engineering manager ..... siting of the main engine [was] a very critical thing too. And Mr Hendry Innes, he was the foreman dockside engineer and it was another nice experience when he showed me the fitting o' the propeller, getting the communications from inside the shaft tunnel to the staging on the outside, and getting the keyway and the propellers all in line. .....

~ ~ ~ ~ ~

Ian McLeod: Johnston mentioned Davie Hay, the shipwright foreman. ..... I was working wi' two shipwrights who'd come over from Leith, ... the shipwright and his labourer, I should say, and they were the greatest dodgers I've ever come across in that yard, and there were some dodgers in that yard. But they had this wee howff[7] right down in the stern o' this boat, and they always had tea going. There was always, and people knew that. And there was this, I cannae remember his name, but he came from either Cowdenbeath or Kelty, another shipwright and he was working on the boat next door. He came down the, what do you call these things, that held the staging up? The uprights?

Tom Allan: Aye, the uprights.

---

[7] Haunt; enclosed space.

The Boilermakers' Squad. BHT collection.

Back row - J. Mudie, J. Mackie, G. Curtis, W. Cruickshanks, G. Burrel, D. Reddie, J. Mackay, A. Dingwall,
A Robertson. *Middle row* - E. Masterton, W. McNiven, J. Smith, J. Mackinnon, J. Brown, Bennet Gass, J. Guyan,
J. Wallace, P. Foster, N. Curtis. *Front row* - R. Curtis, W. Mellis, - Woods, R. Wallace, H. Curtis, C. Inglis.

Burntisland riveters 1934. BHT collection.

Back row - W. Kane, J. Douglas, D. Pringle, G. Stuart, W. Richardson, J. Craig, H. Marsh, W. Maxwell,
B. Dempsey, E. Holmes, C. Proud, F. Gordon, B. Roxburgh, R. Beaston, D. Robertson, G. Watson, H. Anderson.
Middle row - E. McGregor, W. Anderson, S. Tiernan, T. Donnally, F. Quinn, R. Rough, W. Douglas, W. Ferguson,
C. Campbell, T. Nielson, D. Stewart, - Thomas. *Front row* - P. Erskine, R. Grubb, J. Cameron, A. McLean, W. Grieve,
T. Henderson, C. Dickson, D. Burgess (Foreman), D. Canning (Deputy Foreman), W. Bruce, A. Preson, A. Plews,
J. Abie, D. Gillespie, C. Clark.

Burntisland Shipyard Drawing Office Football Select from around 1938.
Back Row - A. Lyle, J. Robertson, A. Simpson, F. Dundas, G. Woodburn, A. Clark.
Front Row - W. Bell, J. Gray, D. Grant, D. McAinsh, G. Henderson.
BHT collection.

Ian McLeod: He came down one upright, stepped across and into the other boat, sitting there having a sip of tea from the can when somebody shouted, "Davie Hay's on board!" ..... Well, [the shipwright] just dropped everything, up this upright, got to the top, realised it was the wrong upright! There was no way he could get back onto the boat he was supposed to be on and Davie Hay appeared at the scene, just stood, looked him straight in the eye; the guy, back down, up the right one, head down and away!

~ ~ ~ ~ ~

Johnston Wood: ..... When number three berth, which was a very exposed position and I remember, it was quite funny, we had several days of easterly winds, snow, sleet, rain, day after day, and I was going down the yard and the foreman said to me, "Mr Wood did you hear about the fight at the bottom of number three berth this morning?" I said, "No." He said, "One o' the men was attacked by a polar bear!"

~ ~ ~ ~ ~

Bill Strawn: Well, in the shipwright department, I was working wi' them, under the big crane. This is the cantilever crane, they used to call it 'the big one'. There was the shipwrights' howff underneath it, and it was divided into two bits by a central wall, but the central wall only come up to about that height. There was a space between the roof and the top o' the wall, and you had two sets o' shipwrights, and they were very competitive. And in this building was two 'H' beams, supports. So they had a competition, and ..... there was one chappie on one side, Jock Graham, and they ca'ed him 'The Horse'. Now the reason they ca'ed him 'The Horse' was he could, if anybody had any sandwiches that was left after lunchtime, he used to eat them. "Jock, you wanting a sandwich?" So he was a champion on, say, the right hand side. So they says, "We'll have a wee competition. We'll see how many times you can grab this beam and pull

114

yourself up with it." So I don't know who the champion was on the left hand side, but here they go, they started off. Up and down, up and down, maybe say about thirty times. "Come on, Jock! Get goin', get goin'!" "I cannae make it!" "Come on, keep goin'!" I think he got about thirty times, thirty, maybe say forty times, and he was absolutely shattered. But he lost, because the other chap managed to get forty-one. But unknown to Jock, the boys are below the other chappie, heaving him up and down!

~ ~ ~ ~ ~

Tom Allan: ..... Tam Lawrence was talking about Jock Roxburgh, he was a man that had a lot o' hens at home, and during the dinner break, hi'self and his son, wee Alec, a wee bowdy-leggit boy, used to go round and pick up a' the crusts and bits o' bread that everybody had thrown away, and put them on top o' the furnace to dry. And then he took them home and broke them a' up to help to feed his hens. And he used to bring in the eggs every day and sell the eggs during the wartime to the men that worked in the shipyard. He went around wi' his bag and a' the crusts and bits o' bread or anything was picked up.

Launching the Ships

Tom Allan: Would it no' be a good thing to maybe get Bill to explain, the slipways, you know, for launching the boat, putting the slips, the ways in, could you maybe explain it better? Like what the carpenters had to do to build up the slips, a' the work, and it maybe only took a couple o' minutes or three minutes for the boat to slide doon, but they'd worked on them for three or four weeks.

Bill Strawn: Well, I was never involved in that, I canny mind, in the loft, in these days, but I'm just going back to what I used to dae in later life, when I worked along in St Monans. We had the same situation and we had to ..... get a certain declivity for the launch ways to go in, in comparison to the declivity o' the ground, which meant that the loft, the ways, the standing ways, that the sliding ways were put on, would be higher up off the ground at the fore end o' the ship, probably, to lower down at the after end. And then, they used to build these up, and then, the men, when these were built up, they used to come in with the sliding ways and they put the sliding ways in, as Bob mentioned, the tallow and everything, to pull them up and that was like a wee village underneath the boat, they guys working, the shipwrights. And it was Willie Peggs and .....

Alex Ferguson: Jim Henderson.

Tom Allan: Ramsay Leslie.

Bill Strawn: These were the two shipwrights that ..... a' the time they used to pull these ways up, and memories from these days was pinching some o' the soft soap, to take hame wi' us, it was fabulous stuff at that time!

Ian McLeod: The soft soap, the tallow was acting as a lubricant between the ways.

Bill Strawn: Ah-ha, but you had the soft soap itself at the time, it was magic stuff at the time. Pull, used to pull these up and then the shipwrights would put in the wedges and everything to bash them in. And how I explain it to people that, when they put they wedges in and the shipwrights come afterwards and used the rams to ram the wedges up, you were actually lifting the ship off the blocks, and the shores that the ship was getting built on. And another memory, if I can go back to when they were launching the ship, is Andy Nichol used to be under the boat, used to knock all the old shores out, and then knock all the blocks out, and the centre o' the ship, you used to leave the blocks on the outside of the ship on. But all the blocks up the keel, Andrew used to say, "Get these out!" and it always happened to fall to the apprentice shipwrights to hit out the steel blocks. Now the steel blocks were like a jigsaw puzzle to me, and the pin that went through them ..... when they married up with all the blank bits in that jigsaw puzzle, this thing used to spring and we used to tap it and tap it and Andrew Nichol would say, "Hit the bloody thing, laddie! Hit the bloody thing!" and you used to hit it and run for your life! And then, that's what you used to hear, the women, even my wife, they used to ..... stand at the Half Moon, you used to hear a' the blocks coming out, the blocks coming out, and then the bell ringing, and then that was it, the boat went down.

Ian McLeod: Ah-ha. The thing about, you mentioned about declivity and so on, but the thing about launches there was that it was a very narrow distance across, so you had to have these drag chains to swing .....

Bill Strawn: That's right. That's right, and another job when I was an apprentice shipwright, they used to have the drag chain on the side o' the boat and ..... there was a pin inside they had to take out, and that was when, I think it was when the ship was pulled round; this chain had the effect of pulling the ship round a wee bit in the restricted area, and once it was round ....., "Get that pin out, laddie!" And you used to put the pin out and the big, like a shackle, used to come out and used to drop off the chains. So the jobs of the apprentice shipwright was manifold, you done everything.

Ian McLeod: As far as I can recollect, the joys, the jobs of any apprentice! I remember getting stuck in an awful airshaft thing, vent shaft, welding a galvanised pipe, nightmare. I ended up wi' these ice, sort o' like icicles from the galvanised stuff on, oh, horrible.

Alex Ferguson: I used to get the galvy flu off o' that. Next day you felt like you had the flu wi' what used to come off the galvaniser.

Ian McLeod: Aye, horrible stuff.

Bob Miller: And these launch ways, Bill, they had the standing way and the sliding way. And, of course, the ship was intended to go straight down the ways, and all they had on the outboard side of the standing way was about an inch of an upstand .....

Bill Strawn: A wee keeper, aye.

Bob Miller: ...... toprevent the ship from going port or starboard.

Bill Strawn: Course the idea was they put the shores in when the ship went down, seemingly, well we know when the ship went down, when it was going down the ways, the tendency wi' the weight o' the ship was to push the ways out, so that was why there was an awful lot o' shores pointing towards the centre o' the ship to stop the standing ways from pulling out.

Johnston Wood: Talking about the launch ways, that was one of the highlights of being in the drawing office, you got out to see the launch, and you were expected to come back wi' some information, something that you had learned, the triggers, or the construction o' the ways or the fore poppets, something like that. And even going to the Green Isle to the stern and timing the launch, you had the length o' the ship and the time, so you could work out the speed and acceleration. ..... the drawing office was a pretty strict disciplined place. The big highlight o' the year was Christmas Day when we got a two hour lunch break, otherwise your head was down all the time. And we worked Saturday mornings and of course, I've seen a draughtsman getting reprimanded by Mr Hall for putting his jacket on one minute before twelve o'clock.

Ian McLeod: You mentioned 'poppets' there, the fore poppets. Could you explain that .....

Johnston Wood: Yeah, well, when the ship was launched, when the stern became buoyant it lifted up and the pressure, or the weight o' the ship, was then transferred to the bow. And there was a downward pressure on the ways, so there was a special reinforcement built up because the ship at the bow was very fine and there was a special arrangement of keel blocks and wedges and everything to take the weight ..... and it was quite alarming when the ship went down and the stern lifted and the weight o' the whole ship came down on the fore poppet, ... sometimes they splintered and broke adrift, but wi' the momentum o' the ship it carried on and was safely in the water. In fact, one o' my first jobs when I went outside to the dock, Mr Clough sent me out in welly boots into the mud harbour because the ship that had just been launched, there wasn't sufficient water, and the sliding way on the starboard side had touched the mud and got stuck, which pushed out the whole sliding way the length o' the ship, and dislodged the fore poppet. ..... then, the ship took a roll, but, as I say, it was moving and it was safely launched. So I had to go out, and I found that the mud had been disturbed by the ways, but there was no disturbance caused by the ship itself, there was no damage at all.

Ian McLeod: One of the things, as an apprentice, I always really wanted to do, was go down with the ship at the launch, not go down with the ship any other way, but go down on the launch. Have any of you here gone on board? What was it like then on this, suddenly, this thing that's been static for so long, starts to move, slowly then faster and faster? Or were you too busy? .....

Bill Strawn: I think you were too busy, because you werenae standing idle. If you were on the boat at the after end they had a series of ropes ..... the rope from the after end that went off the ship, round a block, I think, on the Green Isle and it was attached to a steam crane. Now when the side chains was thrown off the boat, it was getting pulled around, you had to pull on this rope, and at the same time you were pulling on the rope and the crane was actually pulling the rope as well. It was to tighten the rope up to stop her from going, ken, round the corner. And I can always mind that steam crane pulling that rope and us trying to pull it to shorten it a' the time. You're working a' the time on it, you werenae standing, unless you were at the top. Another job that a young apprentice got was when the bottle was burst, you had to pull in the rope for the end o' the bottles and .....

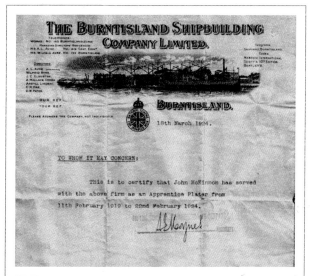

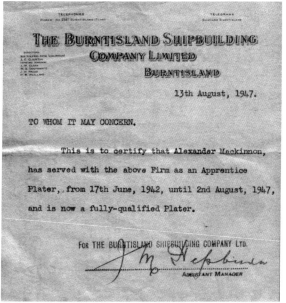

Top - the letter confirming that John Mackinnon had completed his apprenticeship as a Plater in 1924. Bottom - John's son, Alex, followed in the family tradition in 1947. (Alex' brother, Willie, also worked in the shipyard.) Collection of the late Alex Mackinnon.

Tom Allan: You got to lick the rope after you pulled it up! .....

Johnston Wood: Yes, I remember, one o' the jobs for the office boy in the drawing office was to take the champagne bottle down and hitch it onto this rope that you were talking about and it was put on by a clip, quick release, and you had to stand there, holding the bottle, until the launch party came down and it was handed over to the sponsor, and then she christened the ship and smashed the bottle. And your job then was to leap forward and grab the bottle before it was whipped away up.

Bill Strawn: I always heard stories about shipwrights lying on their back wi' their mouth open! I've yet to see it.

Other Reminiscences

Alex Ferguson: Oh, that's when the policeman was doon there, Sergeant, what did they cry him? He was the first aid man/security. And they put green awnings on one o' the boats. I dae ken if you mind aboot that, it was like green corrugated stuff and there was a bit lying, and it was aboot three, two and half feet by aboot three feet. And I looked at this and I'm saying to myself, "That would dae my garden hut for the windae." So I lifted it, I ta'en it round and I put it in the back of my car and he must have seen me. So at finishing time, he come roond and he got a haud o' me and he spoke about it, and I say, "Aye," and he told me to take it oot the car and put it back where I got it. So I done that, I lifted it oot the back o' the car, I went back roond the dockside and I laid it doon. And it was a day or two later he got a haud o' me, I was working in the shed, in number four shed, and he come roond, he said, "Aye, how're ye getting on?" I said, "Fine." He said, "Did you have a use for that piece o' awning, ye ken, the corrugated sheeting?" I telt him what it was I was gonna dae wi' it. He said, "If you come roond and see me," he says, "I'll give you a line for it ..... and you can take it and show it to the gateman when you go oot wi' the piece o' the sheeting," this awning, the green stuff, ye ken, like fibreglass. So I went away roond to him and I got the line fae him and I went back and I got it, put it in the car. And he come roond the next day, he said, "All right?" I said, "Aye." He said, "The next time, ... instead of going and lifting it, ... come and see me ..... and we'll see if it's no needed ..... and we'll give you a line." And that was the piece o' awning. It's actually still on my garden hut yet! But he was just letting me see that he was doing his job, which was quite right. I mean, it was a wee bit and it was just a cutting and I thought to mysel', "Well, they'll no be dae'in much wi' that," but he just showed me that there was a place and time and you had to do things right, and that was it. I forget his name now. ..... McKay, McKay. .....

~ ~ ~ ~ ~

Ian McLeod: ..... a wee anecdote ..... talking about Geordie Rae, Dod Rae. Well, I didn't know the man very well, I was more with people like charge hands and so on like that, but the one thing was that when I got a place at art college, eventually I had to go and see Geordie Rae. And so I went up to his box, and I said, "Can you get my books made up for Friday, because I'm leaving?" And he said, "What do you mean you're leaving? Where are you going?" And I said, "Art college," and he said, "Oh, aye, ... well it's just as well you came to see me, because you were getting paid off on Friday anyway." Simply because I wisnae attending very well in the last wee while, because I knew I was going to art college and I'd lost all interest.

~ ~ ~ ~ ~

Tom Lawrence: What I fault them for, is we were young men, no long married. We'd loved to have bought a house, but there was no sign o' stability. We never knew there was going to be another order, till you saw plates coming in wi' another number on it. When you saw another number, "Oh, I've got another order!" That was, they kept you in the dark all the time. Now at that time, that was the beginning of people beginning to pay up washing machines and all this sort of thing. And being old fashioned, I suppose, we didnae want to do this until we could pay it. Wi' the result is, I know one person, a welder, that took the chance and he's got his own bungalow, up the back. But you were always uncertain.

~ ~ ~ ~ ~

Tom Lawrence: And it was thick, it was thick, sometimes when you had a candle, and oh, gee, the grease used to fall down and when you were welding onto the bottom o' the ship, a' the sections, the smell. And you'd be in there and it would be thick and rather than crawl from here

118

A group of shipyard employees from the 1960s. Collection of the late Alex Mackinnon.

to the other end o' the library, you'd have your piece and your sandwich down there. I mean, half the welders are dead now. I'm no surprised. I think what saved me is I didn't go in for a' the overtime that God sent. I preferred to be doon the harbour, mucking aboot wi' ma boat, getting fresh air.

~ ~ ~ ~ ~

Alex Ferguson: See what Tom's saying there aboot the tank top, I wisnae long in there wi' Billy Roy and Billy Roy got a job doing the tanks, and he said, "We're goan doon here. Have you got a' the gear?" and you gi'en him a hand. I mind o' crawling through at the back o' him, and I mind o' goin' doon this manhole, eighteen inches by a foot, on the tank top. We went doon and we crawled for ages through, putting a' the stuff through and a' the rest o' it, and he used to say to you, "Go and change my juice," and you crawled a' the way back. And at that time, it was a riveted tank top. And I mind o' crawling a' the way up, looking up a' the time, looking up, looking up for this big hole, and I must have crawled up and doon that tank as often, trying to get this manhole. And you no mind the plate they used to put on the top o' the hinge in case somebody fell doon?

Tom Lawrence: Aye, they'd a flap on it.

Alex Ferguson: Well, somebody had flapped the lid doon, and I didnae hae a clue and I was getting to the stage where I went back and Billy Roy said, "Changed my juice?" I said, "No, I canny get oot the tank," and he sat and looked and laughed at me. And I said, "I cannae, ... the hole's no there noo." .....

Tom Allan: Somebody'd welded it up.

Alex Ferguson: He said, "Leave it the noo," and we come oot thegither and 'bang', he just shoved the lid up, but you couldnae stand up and look round about, you just had to keep turning your heid up to see whaur the hole wis. And my knees wis sair, crawling up and doon through a' they holes and I was trying to count the spaces where we were and a' the rest o' it and it was somebody had just shut the lid doon. And I was still looking for this hole that wisnae there.

Tom Lawrence: This lid, by the way, was put on to stop people falling in the manhole. It had maybe two or three holes punched in, but it was on a, it was welded onto a hinge .....

Alex Ferguson: When you see the hole, you thought it was still part o' the tank top wi' the rivets.

The End of the Road: the 'Ohrmazd'

Pictured above is the 'Ohrmazd', built for the East & West Steamship Company of Karachi, Pakistan. Her keel was laid on 13 May 1966. She was launched on 25 April 1967, and delivered to her owners on 2 November 1968. BHT collection.

Tom Lawrence: The 'Pakistani' was the last gasp, because we had the midship section, it was all planned out in Geneva, seemingly, and we got a midship section and we had no idea what sort of bow or stern was going on it, and she was huge. They say she was about 9,000 or 10,000 tons, but I reckon she was away aboot twelve. And once things started moving, this big bulbous bow started forming, away back in number two hold. It was like a big cigar, the frames a' came up and worked round this thing, and I actually welded the inside o' that bulbous bow. It was a huge thing, huge thing. And the bilge keels, usually the bilge keels were long straight bars to stabilise the ship fae rolling. The bilge keels on the 'Pakistani', were snaked, and I asked the, it was a German supervisor, at the time, I asked him at the time, the reason for this, and he said that the bow wave of the bulbous bow, it caused the flow at a certain speed. I think it was away about fifteen or eighteen knots or something, and this would create no resistance. .....

~ ~ ~ ~ ~

Alex Ferguson: ..... the man that was getting the boat built, he was Pakistani, and his name, the nickname they gave him was 'Me no like'. Because, everything that was done, he never liked it. And I mind one time, when it was finished round in the dock, it was gonnae carry immigrants an' a'. And they had the big rice boilers, and because the rice boilers couldnae boil the rice quick enough, it got chucked o'er at the dock and they got other boilers in. And, oh, he was an awfy man. He cost the shipyard its future, actually.

Ian McLeod: But was that not because of the kind of contract?

Tom Lawrence: It was the contract.

Alex Ferguson: It was an open-ended contract.

Tom Lawrence: 'To the owner's satisfaction'. That was the end clause, 'to the owner's satisfaction', and I was Chairman o' the Boilermakers at the time, and I always remember, I went up to see John from Aberdeen, John Wright, and he was crying like a kid. He says, "Gentlemen," he says, "I've called you up here to tell you that we're going into liquidation." And I blame the

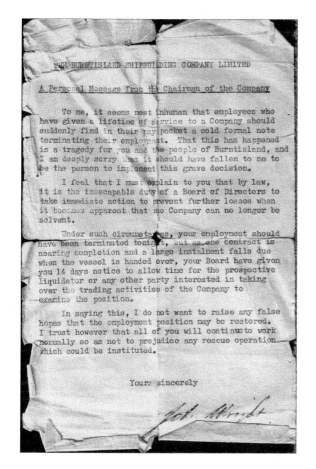

The letter from John Wright which was sent out to the shipyard employees, confirming that their employment was being terminated. Collection of the late Alex Mackinnon.

management for no jumping on that man as soon as things started going wrong. Because ..... he had the ship outside, he didnae have a contract, and the ship lay out there with a' the carpenters on board, for insurance purposes, he didn't have a crew. His wife got a sore head, she sent ashore for aspirins and charged them to the shipyard. A bottle o' aspirins and charged them to the shipyard, that's how bad it was. And then, when he got a contract, there was a crew on board right away, and she was away. Now the first contract was sulphate, and sulphate, I've spoken to seamen that have handled this stuff, when it gets damp, it goes like cement. And sometimes they've to bore holes and blow it adrift and he tried to bring a claim against the yard that the ship was leaking, causing the sulphate to, you know. And it went from one thing to another and then I believe she got, somebody put limpet bombs on her, out in some foreign port, in the Middle East someplace and sunk her.

Alex Ferguson: As Tom says, on that boat, when she was finished, we were a' watching her going oot that day for her trial up and doon the Forth, and actually, it was supposed to be in the port, but she disappeared one weekend, and he had her away doon the east coast. And she come back up, and then she come back in again, because there was stuff on it he didnae like. I think she was in once or twice, Tam, 'cause one time she damaged herself on the pier coming in, and when they got it a' sorted, they altered the anchor pockets for him, they done this and that, and I think it was the third time she went oot, they said, "No way is that ship coming back into Burntisland." Every time she came in it was costing the yard money to alter something, every time.

~ ~ ~ ~ ~

Bob Miller: ..... the one who will never be forgotten, I'm sure, in everybody's mind here, was one Pakistani gentleman called Argisheer Kavasji. And he was the owner of, or to be the owner of, ship number 418. ..... And there was no one, from a ship owner's point of view, who could ever compare with Mr Kavasji. ..... he got to the point where previously in dealing with all the other directors they couldn't control him any longer, and I was then given to him as being his contact with changes, and of course he wanted many.

And that was much to the dissatisfaction of the whole shipyard and I became, well, close to Kavasji, not that that's a position one would want to be in for a number of years, but I was and you therefore form a relationship one to the other. He would take me out to the ships on the building berths and to the ship when it got into the water and he was showing me the items with which he was unhappy, and which I had to come back to the office and discuss with him and so on. And he didn't let me alone, he had several words he used to describe me and he would use them quite forcibly at times, because I wasn't naturally always in agreement with him, rather the reverse. .....

I think he originally said that Howard Johnson had sold him a chicken and tried to talk it into a hen, in relation to the ship that he was getting as opposed to that which he thought he was going to get. And he was a very clever man, Kavasji, of course, and the contract which the builders had undertaken, had been taken on at the time when we were short of orders, and it's difficult to blame anyone for the scenario. But they did sign a contract with him which asked for his ship, a high-class cargo/passenger liner, built to the highest European shipbuilding standards. And these clauses were left in the contract, which most of the men in the yard didn't see, but they were the mainstay of his whole case, in relation to all the changes he was asking us to make.

But I can only conclude that those who were responsible for undertaking the contract were unaware of what he was going to do to them. I mean 'high class shipbuilding standards' are the highest in Europe. Now, Burntisland couldn't rise to that level. Apart from anything else, Burntisland priced their ships on what Burntisland built, which were more or less normal, but varied types of cargo ships. And the directors who signed the contract must have concluded, "Well, what's wrong with our high class European standards?" but it didn't meet the requirements of the contract.

..... the liquidators, who are appointed when a business goes into debt, appointed me General Manager, to take control of everything.

This is a poem written when the fight was on to save the shipyard. The author is unknown.
It has been slightly edited. BHT collection.

SAVE BURNTISLAND

0h Burntisland, freenly toon,
Has everybody let us doon?
Ever since we heard the news,
We've voiced opinions, voiced our views.
The fight is on - an' we'll fight hard
Fur somebody tae save oor Yard.
But naebody, it seems, wants tae ken.
We've even been tae Wedgwood Benn:
A head man in the British Nation,
He met oor Union deputation.
They told him o' the toon's great plight,
0' how we were prepared tae fight.

But why should we, guid Scottish
craftsmen,
Welders, Plumbers, Platers,
Draughtsmen,
Go tae him wi' cap in hand? -
Awa' doon tae a foreign land,
An' ask, "Please Save Us From The
Dole."
Already there's a heavy toll
0' men who've lost their zest for life
In oor wee Kingdom, we call Fife.

As human beings we've a right.

It's time that we a' saw the light.
The Scottish work force is sair depleted;
They gang doon sooth - they're better treated.

This treatment mak's me think its funny
How other people spend oor money.
When other countries seem to crash
Then Wilson sends them plenty cash.
But a' we want is some help here.
0' hard work we've had nae fear.

We shouldnae' hae tae cross the Border:
Just gie us anither order.
Just one chance, that's a' we need -
Just gie us a single lead;
Then we'll show what we can do.
Wan boat soon will lead tae two.

In oor toon there'll be nae strife:
We'll find again oor zest for life.
If someone, somewhere, hears oor plea,
Come tae us an' you'll soon see -
As working men, we are nae fools;
We've got the skills, we've got the tools.
We're craftsmen - we'll no' let ye doon.
We're here, ye see, tae SAVE OOR TOON.

The Last Ship: the 'Helen Miller'

The 'Helen Miller' was built for the St Vincent Shipping Company Ltd. Her keel was laid on 21 March 1968. She was launched on 3 April 1969, and delivered to her owners later that year.

Bob Miller: [The 'Helen Miller'] required to be launched, and ..... that final ship wouldn't leave its building berth, it wouldn't go into the water. We tried to launch it again in the afternoon of the same day, but it wouldn't move again on the sliding ways. Subsequently, it was discovered that whilst we had adopted our usual practices with tallow on the ways and all manner of things, and fires in between the ways ..... They had frozen to the point that the ship couldn't slide, and the ship had then to be, well virtually, jacked off these ways, the ways all removed and then all re-tallowed and greased and re-mounted under the ship. And the owner's people came back for the final launch, which was a complete success. But that was a very drastic and dramatic event for all of us in the yard. That day everybody felt under some blame for the failure to launch, but it wasn't really, it was an imbalance of nature. ..... it seemed significant, everybody had their own thoughts about it.

Ian McLeod: Maybe it didn't want to leave.

Bob Miller: It came down to nothing, but it may have been an act of God.

The 'Helen Miller', stuck fast in March 1969. She was successfully launched on 3 April, and delivered to the St Vincent Shipping Company on 14 July. BHT collection.

The late Alex Mackinnon, former shipyard worker like his father before him, recorded these events: "The ship refused to budge when the chocks were removed and despite lighting fires to warm the tallow on the slipways it still would not go and the launch was postponed. It transpired that the actual slipways were not parallel so we had to re-prop the ship, taking the weight off the slipway, realign the runners and then lower the ship down into position again. The launch then went without a hitch." Alex also remembered that, despite the fact that the workforce were working themselves onto the dole queue, they completed the 'Helen Miller' ahead of schedule and received a £20 bonus per man for a job well done.

Other Shipyard Memories

Jimmy Wilson:

Well, this lady, my customer when I was a message boy, or when I used to deliver her orders, her husband was in the dockyard. He was in the office somewhere, and it was him that got me the job as just an ordinary five-eighths labourer. ..... I had to watch what I was doing and watch what other men were doing, and I did the same.

[A five-eighths labourer was] just an ordinary labouring man, just, you did anything or everything that you were asked to do. ..... there was no trade attached to it, you were just a labourer and you went and did, if you were told to go and dig a hole, you went and dug a hole and if you were told to build something up, you built it up, or unloaded lorries, or unloaded wagons, or did anything. We used to have to do a' jobs, a' sorts o' jobs. Once times you had to do a' the drag chains for the anchor, for the launching of the boats, and put them up and down the side of the boat and do a' the things. Lifeboat tests, when they were doing lifeboats. Things like, anything, any job at all that a labourer had to do.

..... at that time, it was never very secure. You were always working, there was always strikes, you were always short time. ..... Heater boys used to come oot if the char wasnae big enough, or it was too big, or something like that, they would be off for a day, or there would be no work for a day. But I never got tae that stage. We were always working. But you just had to, when you got paid off, they didna hang about, if there wasnae any work, you didna get kept on, you got paid off. I mean I was paid off a couple o' times in the shipyard, but I always went and worked somewhere else. Maybe down the docks, stevedoring, down loading alumina for the aluminium or bauxite out the boats and that. ..... that is when I was doing odd jobs, going stevedoring at the docks, on a bauxite boat, or bags of, two hundredweight bags, they were, of alumina. And you had to carry them, and it was a' right carrying them when you were on the hold o' the boat, but as the boat was getting built up, you're walking on bags, and the heat, when you went home at night, your back was red raw, wi' the heat o' the bags. .....

There was always work if you were prepared to go and work. It wasnae like this day and age now, where ye dinnae work and ye still get mair money than what you do when you're working. I mean some o' these young lads that's going aboot the now, they don't know what work is.

Janet Agnew and Sadie Edwards in conversation with Ian Archibald and John Burnett:

Janet Agnew: The earliest memory I have, is coming down to the Half Moon ..... and watching the Prince of Wales coming to the Burntisland shipyard. .....

Sadie Edwards: My father died in '38, so I only had my mother, my mother and I. And then the war broke out, of course, in 1939, so things were very difficult. My sister was ten years older than me and there was a big age gap, and somehow, well my mother had to struggle. In those days there was no social security. Her pension was ten shillings a week, and because she had me ..... it was put up to fifteen shillings, so she had to live on that. Consequently, she took in boarders, lodgers, which half the people in the Castle did. The shipyard was booming, and they had lots and lots of contractors, from Newcastle, from Glasgow, Clydebank; all these people. And there's still traces of them now in Burntisland from the war days. .....

Janet Agnew: Pretty well the same, my mother, even, she took in boarders. We had people that came from Edinburgh, and they came faithfully every year and spent, a family that came from Glasgow and they came every year. It was a struggle, but everybody seemed to manage, I had an older sister, I *have* an older sister, she's, how old is she? Seventy-nine; she'll be seventy-nine next month. No, there was just the two of us. My father worked in the shipyard and he was in the Home Guard. Funnily enough, I just saw the certificate for him. My husband died just recently and I was cleaning out Seth's drawer and here's the certificate of my father being in the Home Guard. I thought it was brilliant.

Ian Archibald: And he was also in the shipyard?

Janet Agnew: Yes he was. He worked there, pretty well until it was closing down, and then he went to Rosyth for a while, but he worked there, he had quite a bad accident down there. He was a football coupon collector and he would go down in the night shift during the war, and he got crushed, his legs got crushed with a crane that was driven by a *woman* and that was terrible! However, he survived it and ..... that was what happened with him.

Sadie Edwards: There was lots of women worked in the shipyard. My sister was a painter, and they had welders. Chris Blackhall? ..... She was a welder in the shipyard, during the war and, oh, lots of women who came from Kirkcaldy, all over.

Janet Agnew: That was one of my memories, waiting for, coming down to meet my father from the shipyard and had an awful job trying to find him, because of the crowds of men and women that came out ..... it was fantastic. It got to the stage where I couldn't go down there, I had to wait at the close ..... because there was too many buses coming and it was tremendous.

Sadie Edwards: That was at the time when I started work. When the shipyard was coming out, ten past five the horn went, there was a queue of buses towards the shipyard, which is under the bridge now. These were the Kirkcaldy buses. Now there must have been ..... a fleet of, about, eight to ten buses. Round the corner where the Dunfermline stop is, there was another fleet of buses, which went ..... up the Dunfermline area. And beyond that there was another fleet of buses, which went to the Cowdenbeath area. That's Cowdenbeath, Bowhill, Lochgelly, Cardenden, we knew all the boys, 'cause they came up the street at lunchtime.

Left - women shipyard workers in the Second World War.
Back Row - Nellie Hutchison, Mima Murray, Alice Maddison, Mee Williamson, Ina Leuchars, Madelaine Hepburn, Flo Motion, May Wallace, Lizzie Cooper.
Front Row - Madge Webb, Maryanne Donachie, Mrs Hepburn, Bella Spence, Annie Bruce, May Reid.
BHT collection.

Betty Traynor:

My father Joe McNeil and my mother, big sister and wee brother, came through to live in Burntisland in 1921 when I was four years old and we lived in Union Street down from Möller's shop. My dad came to work in the shipyard, which hadn't long started. He worked as a hole borer/caulker, as they called it in those days, and his job was drilling out holes for the rivets to go into to join up parts of the ship. He worked in the Burntisland shipyard all of his working life and became a chargehand.

Chapter 6

The Railway

The façade and principal offices of Burntisland's original railway station still dominate Forth Place. They date from 1847, when the Burntisland to Cupar section of the Edinburgh and Northern Railway opened. The Cupar to Ferry-Port-on-Craig section was opened the following year, completing the trans-Fife connection between the Forth and Tay ferries.

Above - the 1847 station building. J.L. Stevenson collection.

William Erskine, in his 1930 book, 'Glimpses of Modern Burntisland', commented on the old station buildings: "The station itself was much the same as it still is, the polished stone portico with its weather-worn pillars forming the western front. Otherwise it was innocent of any pretension to elegance, the projectors of it having designed the buildings for utility rather than as a model of aesthetic taste. The old ticket or booking-office is now utilised as a dwelling-place for railway servants, and, of course, the span of the station roof has gone the way of most earthly things. The row of low buildings formerly used for miscellaneous purposes still remains, neglected and pointless, a testimony to the economical tendencies of railway management. Even the good old 'Bar', which resounded often with the desperate cries of thirsty and semi-famishing travellers, and where sweet and attractive young ladies supplied the demand, has lost its virtue, and may now be the home of the rodents, upon whose heads or tails hygienic authorities have set a price. A foreign mission station occupies an adjoining room, and it is understood that the space therein provides ample accommodation for all that maybe attracted to it."

There was, until fairly recently, a plaque on the wall in Forth Place, commemorating the inauguration of the world's first roll on/roll off ferry in 1850. This was a rail ferry, with the fully loaded coal waggons being run directly onto the ship.

Until the opening of the Forth Bridge in 1890, Burntisland was a terminus of national significance. In that period, the Burntisland/Granton ferry was the principal means of crossing the Forth estuary. Passengers transferred from the train to the ferry, and back to the train at the other side. After 1890 the ferry diminished in importance, but Burntisland continued as a major coal exporting port for many years.

In 1890, the original station was superseded by a decidedly modest and undistinguished through station on the adjoining site to the north. That station still serves the town.

The Control in Forth Place

The railway Control building had a long and distinguished history, but its demolition in 1997 became inevitable after a period of shameful neglect.

The original building on the site was the parish manse, built about 1823-24. It was an early work by the prolific architect, William Burn (1789-1870). Burn specialised in country houses, designing about 150 in total, including Falkland House, Balcarres House, Balintore Castle and Tynninghame.

The prospect of the arrival of the railway provided the opportunity for the old manse building to be extended and converted into the Forth Hotel around 1845-47, with the Church of Scotland relocating to a new manse in Cromwell Road (now Grayforth House nursing home).

The last proprietor of the Forth Hotel was the colourful character, James Louden. Born in Hillend in 1848, he started his working life as a ship's carpenter. He became a railway engineer, working in Sri Lanka and Trinidad. He was involved in the construction of the Forth Bridge, almost losing his life in an accident just before the opening in the 1890.

Retiring from engineering, he took over the Forth Hotel in Burntisland in 1903 and ran it until his death in 1914. His niece, Ann McCall (also the proprietor of The Green Tree Tavern in the High Street), took over until the lease expired in 1917.

Around 1920, the Forth Hotel was converted to the Burntisland railway Control, which is how the building is best remembered in the town today. It controlled train movements in an area stretching to Bridge of Earn and Montrose to the north and Causewayhead (near Stirling) to the west, and southbound trains as far as the Forth Bridge. It eventually became British Rail's District Operating Administrative Office, although to local folk it remained simply 'The Control'.

In 1965 the superintendents, clerks and typists were relocated to Edinburgh, and complete closure followed five years later. Very precisely, at 10.00 p.m. on Sunday 1 February 1970, the Burntisland Control ceased to be - as did equivalent operational centres at Aberdeen and Edinburgh Waverley, all subsumed in the new Edinburgh Waverley Communications Centre.

The building was put on a care and maintenance basis, looked after by the local station staff. In due course it was sold to a building company. Plans were put forward to convert it to flats, but they came to nothing. The fabric was now deteriorating rapidly, and in 1993 the local authority suggested that the site be used for a 'park and ride' facility - this also came to nothing. By 1997 the old hotel had decayed to such an extent that it had to be demolished. A new block of flats was recently erected on the site.

Top - the Forth Hotel around 1900, from James Louden's notepaper. Bottom - the same building, photographed in 1989, eight years before demolition. Iain Sommerville collection.
At the time of the Coronation of Edward VII in 1902, the Forth Hotel was described as "the best decorated building in Burntisland". Ann McCall remembered years later that the hotel was "a riot of colour: red, white and blue, all entwined around the door pillars".

Jim Calder and Bill Cook, in conversation with Ian Archibald and John Wright, recall the days when they worked in the Burntisland Control:

Jim Calder: ..... we worked together at times, because we were at different jobs, we mighta been on different shifts. You must remember this place was open every day of the year.

Ian Archibald: We're talking about the Control room. Can we say what the Control room did? What was the purpose o' the Control room?

Jim Calder: Well, all it did was try to keep the traffic moving and get the traffic from A to B, in connection wi' a working timetable ..... the working timetable was the timetable for all the trains that run through the area. And Burntisland was a district of the railway, and in Scotland, you had Aberdeen, Perth, Edinburgh and Glasgow. That was the areas. ..... Very few people in Burntisland, I found, knew anything about the Control. [Local folk said that] everybody worked in the Control. Now that's not true. Only a certain fraction o' the staff worked in the Control ..... everybody in Burntisland thought that that building was the Control. It wasn't, it was the District Office. It was the District Operating Superintendent. It was ..... the operating side o' the railway. And there was all these, all the different departments were there that you had in Edinburgh and Glasgow, all the different departments; they were maybe not as big ..... they used to say, "He worked in the Control," [but] he maybe worked in the staff, he maybe worked in a passenger train station, as long as he worked in that building ..... this was the Head Office, but on the operating side of the railway. It had nothing to do with the commercial side at all, or the engineering side, come to that, ... so far as that district was concerned. .....

Bill Cook: Mind you, having said that, there was how many staff ....., Jim? There was nine on a shift, ... nine, ten, day shift and back shift. ..... Sixty, aye, sixty, sixty-five, Jim? Sixty to sixty-five of a staff in the whole of the office down there? .....

Jim Calder: But [it] was quite a big building; you had the plant as well. ..... I mean, all together, probably, the Control had half the staff, maybe.

Bill Cook: Yes, I would say that.

Jim Calder: About half the staff were in the Control, but everybody, everybody said that if they worked in that building, they worked in the Control, which was not true.

Bill Cook: Aye, that's right. It was mainly goods traffic we did the moving of, if the passenger trains ran to time.

Jim Calder: Well, of course, [we had] passenger-train controllers as well. .....

~ ~ ~ ~ ~

Bill Cook: The Control was closed in January 1970. Aye.

Jim Calder: That's right. We had the place to ourselves for four years.

Bill Cook: That's right. And then when it closed, we were moved to Edinburgh.

Railway Economics

Ian Archibald: When you're talking about the passenger trains and the goods trains, we're talking about an era when the railways, nearly everything was moved by goods.

Jim Calder: Well, yes, because the railway were common carriers. Railways were what you called common carriers, in other words, they couldn't refuse traffic, anything. ..... it was a joke if ye saw what they charged. I mean, I worked on the commercial before I went on the Control and ..... for example, a man wanted a horse taken from Falkirk, I was working in Falkirk Grahamston, and he wanted it taken to Bellgrove. It didnae walk. So we had to order a horsebox for that, he got it to the plant, and [at] the plant, they said, "Right, we've got a horsebox at Larbert." Now you had to take that horsebox from Larbert to Falkirk Grahamston. ..... The man came, loaded the horse, then an engine had to take it and put it on the back o' a train. It went to

Cowlairs, because Bellgrove is on the low-level side o' Glasgow, it went to Cowlairs, it stopped at Cowlairs. They unhooked it off the back, got an engine and a guard and run down to Bellgrove with it, and the cost was twelve shillings and tenpence. ..... It was hopeless, absolutely hopeless, it was quite evident what was going to happen. It's a wonder they lasted as long.

Jim Calder: ..... some o' the rates that they charged were ridiculous. ..... you could have parcels collected, we'll say at Thurso, up in John O' Groats, somewhere ..... It was only a wee parcel, it was going to Falmouth, or somewhere in Cornwall, it was in about six different trains, it was sixpence! It was a tanner! They'd be better just throwing them in the fire.

Bill Cook: Mind you, on the passenger side, they used to have, what was called, if you were travelling by train for your holidays, you got your luggage collected for two and fourpence. So if you and your family were going for a holiday from, we'll say, as Jim said, we'll say Inverness to London, you could have your luggage collected for two and fourpence per trunk. You get that collected at the house and it's delivered wherever you're going to in London because you were travelling by train. And if it was only one way, if you took the luggage to your station at Inverness, and had it delivered in London, it was only one and tuppence. ..... Oh, aye, they used to have a special train going along the east o' Fife collecting luggage at the Fair fortnight. Collected luggage, yes. What we call 'CL' for Collected Luggage, or Delivered Luggage. You couldn't get your luggage free from Inverness to London by taking it to the station at Inverness and collecting it at London, you still had to pay one and tuppence. .....

Jim Calder: Oh, there was a lot o' anomalies on the railway, there was a train ran from Edinburgh to Caldercruix, this side o' Airdrie. ..... And this train, you know, it was just [for the General Manager of a paper mill], the train was only run for him. Nobody was in it, it was that time o' day when there was nobody travelling at all!

Coal waggons in the sidings adjacent to the East Dock in 1931. The large structures beyond the sidings are the dock's coal hoists. J.L. Stevenson collection.

Coal Traffic

Bill Cook: But if passenger trains ran to time, Jim, all we did was goods traffic, and that was our main function.

Jim Calder: Oh, that's right, and it was coal traffic we had. ..... ninety per cent o' the work that was done was wi' coal.

Bill Cook: Yes. You had to make sure you had enough empties in Seafield and all the pits, for them to load. Then you had to get them out, then get more empties in.

Ian Archibald: So ..... you were controlling the output from the pits, determining where it was going.

Bill Cook: That's right. ..... it went to Thornton yard. Most of it went to Thornton yard.

Ian Archibald: Where was the coal going?

Bill Cook: At that time, it was shipping from Methil and down to Battersea Power Station in London.

Jim Calder: Aye, actually, a lot o' the traffic, the coal traffic that come out o' the pits didn't go to a master yard at all. It ..... was destined for, say, the West o' Scotland, in which case it went to Cadder yard, which is at Lenzie. ..... So if it was traffic for the West o' Scotland, more or less, it ..... nearly all went to Cadder yard. ..... you didn't take it to Thornton, for the simple reason, you maybe had a train starting from Inverkeithing or Townhill or wherever, and they used to take the traffic to Lumphinnans Central or Cowdenbeath South where there was sidings, and they were picked up from there and put on a train to Cadder. .....

Bill Cook: Depends which pits they come out.

The Burntisland Control Responsibilities

Jim Calder: ..... it was a very small area, the Burntisland area. It was, compared wi' some o' the big ones, likes in Glasgow. .....

Ian Archibald: So what was the geographical area, Bill, that you were covering?

Bill Cook: The whole of the Control covered from the Forth Bridge, this side of the Forth Bridge to Montrose.

Jim Calder: Stirling, well, start in Montrose, Bridge of Earn going into Perth.

Bill Cook: Bridge of Earn and Causewayhead, wasn't it?

Jim Calder: Then you had Stirling, going to Stirling, Alloa .....

Bill Cook: But Causewayhead was the boundary, wasn't it?

Jim Calder: That's right. ..... Stirling, of course, come under Glasgow, really, but we had still trains going there. And, of course, we had also trains going across the ..... bridge which runs via Throsk, from Alloa, Throsk and over to Larbert. That was a single railway line that went across that bridge.

Ian Archibald: So is it fair to say that Burntisland, really, was quite a nerve centre .....?

Jim Calder: Well, it was, course it was, a' these district offices were nerve centres, but it was only the operating side o' the railway really ..... nothing to do wi' the commercial side and they worked in conjunction wi' the locomotive side, the power side. ..... that was still an office of it's own, the motive power superintendent. So you had the district goods and passenger manager, likes o' our commercial side was Dundee. Our commercial manager was at Dundee. And he was an entirely different outfit altogether. And when Bill worked down at Methil, he was under the district goods and passenger manager at Dundee. Burntisland was nothing to do with him, really.

Bill Cook: Two entirely different departments.

Jim Calder: Exactly. That's right.

Bill Cook: Commercial and operating. Divorced from each other altogether.

Freight Movements

John Wright: Bill, you made mention about keeping the lines clear every day for the fish trains and the meat trains, can you remember?

Bill Cook: Well, that's right. If the fish trains or meat trains were running out of course, you sometimes had to shunt a passenger train to let them through - to give them priority because they were going to London and the passenger trains were maybe just going to Edinburgh .....

passenger trains were classed as 'Class 1', that was an express train; 'Class 2' was the stopping trains; 'Class 3' was fish and meat; and '4' was a fully, what we called a fully braked fitted train. But if the fish or meat trains were running out, we told the signal man to shunt the passenger train to let them through to get, what was called, their 'path' from Edinburgh to the markets in London and that was the meat markets and the fish markets. They were coming from Aberdeen. Two fish trains a day and two meat trains a day. .....

Jim Calder: ..... at first when I went there was only one meat train a day. They were big trains, of course, the big trains. They went to London. ..... [A third fish train ran] when the traffic was heavy.

Left - Burntisland Junction signal box in 1973.

Below- Burntisland railway station in 1955.

J.L. Stevenson collection.

Re-routing

Jim Calder: ..... But another thing about the railway, the Control was there to try and put things right, as Willie says, you shunt a train and so forth, and if you got a derailment, when the line was shut, you couldn't run any trains on it, and you had to make alternative arrangements. For example, you could run trains round via Cowdenbeath instead o' running them via Kinghorn. ..... that's the thing you had to, that happened quite often. ..... so the Control was also there to try and keep the traffic moving as best it could.

Bill Cook: If the main line got blocked, passenger trains were our priority then. The goods trains were just disposed of, really. Aye, you kept the line clear for passengers.

Jim Calder: ..... I'm talking about, 19, the 1950s and before. And after, for a while, you never heard o' a passenger train being cancelled like they are today. Today, you get them all over the railway system. [At] Bathgate there was three cancelled, one after the other, coming out of Bathgate going to Edinburgh. Now you never got that here. ..... I mean, in the old days, that didnae happen, because what you did was, if you were absolutely stuck, you had spare men.

Bill Cook: Well, you cancelled the goods train and used the crew o' the goods train. ..... Used [the] crew for the passenger train.

The Days of Steam

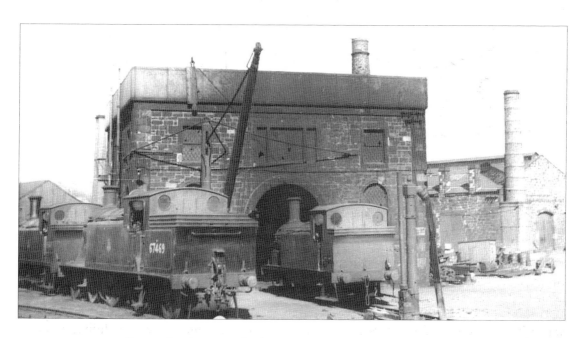

Burntisland engine shed in 1952. J.L. Stevenson collection.

Jim Calder: It was all steam.

Bill Cook: That's up to 1965, I think. Then it was diesel after.

Jim Calder: It started about 1962, I think, ... but they was still mixed, steam trains and diesel trains. But the diesels, of course, made an awful difference. ..... steam engines, I mean, people wouldnae believe how many staff it took to look after railway engines. All the different trades, all the different tradesmen. ..... We dealt with, we spoke to them and we dealt, worked hand in glove with them, we had to because they'd to give us the engines, we'd to ask them for engines ...... you had boys to fill the coal in the bunker, you did that. You had also to fill the tank wi' water. Then you'd to light the fire, and when the day's work was finished you're supposed to draw the fire. ..... you couldnae keep the fire going and the water boiling or you'd run out o' water. ..... I couldnae even tell ye them a' because I never worked in the motive power.

Bill Cook: Some of the motive power depots had what was called a 'caller out' ..... They would go and call out the men for a three o'clock shift and a half past four shift or anything. They went to their houses and called them up. And that was on a regular roster, rota. It's not as if they were getting called out in an emergency.

Jim Calder: ..... Oh, the motive power was expensive ..... the diesels are nothing now, you just fill them up, put the water in and fill them, as long as you put them in the right place, and you didn't want the diesel going in where the water should go, and that has happened.

Ian Archibald: We get the impression, certainly, when you look at the days of steam, that they were very fast trains.

Jim Calder: No, they werenae. They were very slow trains. ..... the good thing about the steam trains, you could run after them when they were leaving the platform, open the door, get on the train and you were in the train before the thing left the end o' the platform, no wi' the diesel.

Burntisland Docks

John Wright: What about the local scene, the movement of trains in Burntisland and Burntisland docks?

Bill Cook: All that was really done at Burntisland docks was the bringing in of ore from Takoradi in West Africa for the Aluminium works.

Jim Calder: ..... the hoists were all there when we came. ..... there were still five coal hoists, and the coal hoists worked on a high level and on a low level. When you were bringing in coal from the pits, they went in on a low level and they were lifted up high, and they were tipped over, hydraulically, and the coal went into the bunkers, coal went into a hold ..... when they were put into the high level, when the wagon was empty, ... it just run down the gradient, so it was never touched again. It had to be lifted up to empty it, but once they were empty, they put it on the high level and it just run down the hill and it used to run into a siding .....

Bill Cook: [The bauxite] came in by boat, then it was by crane grabs, that loaded them into wagons.

Jim Calder: Aye, the old grabs used to take two tons.

Bill Cook: Then they got the bigger.

Jim Calder: Then they got the bigger one, the bigger ones that took five tons.

Bill Cook: And loaded them into wagons and then that was worked by a train from Burntisland yard to the aluminium works. Everything that came in for the aluminium works came to Burntisland yard first .....

Jim Calder: [Transporting bauxite from the docks to the aluminium works by rail] was an expensive business. And of course, they had a contract ..... I think it was a shilling a ton or something like that. This was what they paid for getting the stuff delivered and it was an expensive way o' doing, back and forward, bringing the empties back. And no' only that, it was an awful waste o' wagons, because ..... they used to load the wagons up and put them in a siding, and they didnae take the stuff in ..... the wagons lay in Burntisland Yard.

Bill Cook: They controlled what they wanted into the aluminium works. ..... Mind you, latterly, they were using old condemned wagons that were just kept to main line standard and no more. They weren't used for anything else. Then if they got too bad, they were scrapped down at the scrap yard at Inverkeithing.

Personalities

Bill Cook: Jim eventually moved to Burntisland and stayed. I moved from Buckhaven to stay here. Most people stayed, there was one or two stayed in Thornton. There was one stayed in Aberdour, but then there was the superintendent, who had a chauffeur and a big Humber Snipe. .....

Jim Calder: He was a dandy.

Bill Cook: Jim, Jimmy Dewar. He stayed along Kinghorn Road and he was about six foot, six feet odd tall and his wife was maybe about five feet or something. And he was a rough diamond, Jimmy Dewar, but he knew his work. He knew everybody on the railway.

Jim Calder: He knew Burntisland.

Bill Cook: He knew everybody on his patch. .....

~ ~ ~ ~ ~

Jim Calder: ..... And there was some o' the things that happened on the railway were absolutely unbelievable. I knew a driver that come off an engine with a nanny goat which had been on the banking, the railway banking. He had a bloody nanny goat on the engine. He had a smallholding. But of course, he had to give the man back his nanny goat. But it had strayed onto the railway embankment!

Tragedies

Bill Cook: This night, there was a train driver reported at Kinghorn that there was a body, or something, lying on the line near the monument. So that was reported to us and we had to do the necessary and got the police out and they got rid of the body and ..... the police inspector ..... said to me the next day, "That was an awfy job you sent me oot on, Willie." I says, "Does that no' turn your stomach?" "No, no, no," he says, "you pick up the five bits o' the body, put them in a bag, take them to the mortuary and then it's when you're making a body oot o' this ..... I need a gless o' whisky." .....

Jim Calder: ..... A lot of people committed suicide on the railway. .....

Jim Calder: The worst one I ever remember was a boy down about Barry Links, ... Carnoustie way, and he got hit, but the driver, they know they've hit something, because they say that even on the steam engines, in the days o' steam engines, if somebody put a ha'penny on the line to make it into a penny, to flatten it, the driver knew he'd run over something. And this man, they found bits o' him all the way to Aberdeen. .....

Bill Cook: There was this goods train either coming from Dundee or Aberdeen to Edinburgh, and passing Thornton, just before Thornton station, there was a chap came up from the Methil branch. I don't know if you know the layout there, the main line and the Methil branch, he came up off o' the banking and walked out in front of an engine in a suicide. Now, we had to call out the District Inspector and all the rest of it, and the District Inspector was playing golf on the golf course at Thornton. But there was a message sign put out from the signal box, a great big shirt, or something, put on a shaft ..... you see he was on call, the traffic inspectors were always on call, not every week, took turns, and he went up there and he saw what was happening. So, once the train got to Thornton station, well, the driver had to be relieved, whether he wanted to or not. And Jock Todd, the inspector came into the Control one day and I said, "There'd be some mess, was there no?" "There wasn't a drop o' blood. His chest was pulp."

The Lammerlaws Houses

Bill Cook: ..... The railway was good to me and I benefited from it and eventually I finished up, I retired when I was fifty-six, redundancy and that's twenty-one years retirement.

Ian Archibald: And Jim, you settled down in the Lammerlaws.

Jim Calder: Oh, yes, yes.

Ian Archibald: You told me [once how the Lammerlaws houses were] painted.

Jim Calder: Oh, ... very few people in Burntisland bought any stuff, do-it-yourself stuff. They either go into the shipyard: a boy I played golf wi' told me a' the time he was in the shipyard, he never bought a tin o' paint. ..... I think the shipyard went bust ..... because they stole it. Theyda' stole the damn boats!

Ian Archibald: What about the painting of the houses on the Lammerlaws?

Jim Calder: Oh, it was all railway paint. It was all LNER paint. It was quite good paint. But it was an awful mess, what a place it was. Oh, my goodness, and of course they never repaired the houses, ... they only did what was absolutely necessary. They wernae collecting enough money. I was only paying twenty-five bob a week, which was more than I paid at Bathgate for a modern house, but this was a great big eight-roomed house; [the houses] were all eight rooms, but they had been sub-let. .....

Ian Archibald: The railways owned the Lammerlaws?

Jim Calder: Oh, I think so, yes. And they owned all that ground and everything. When the railway company asked the town to take over, if they would buy the property, and as far as I know, the railway company wanted twenty-five thousand, or something like that. This was 19, in the 60s, in, we'll say, the middle 60s. The railway company wanted about twenty-five thousand for all the houses and all the land. Now the land was quite a lot as well. And then they had the three big houses, Victoria Cottage, Albert Cottage and North View House, which were all big, substantial houses, and so was ours, the five houses we were in; eight rooms, and they were well hardy houses, but they'd never been looked after. ..... the town [council] said, "We'll get our own assessor." ..... And the [council's] assessor valued the property [at a much lower valuation,] and it was a racket. I'm no' going to mention names, but I mean, three of the houses that I know of, they made an agreement. They were never advertised or anything, just people got the houses, people had the houses. Don't know what they paid for them. I suppose there must have been details in the Council records. But how they got the houses, I've no idea. ..... they were going to turn them into ten houses, but it fell through. They found out they could build new houses cheaper, they were building Coltburndale and such places. ..... so they emptied everybody out of their houses. And we were living in the Lammerlaws ourselves and we were in number 5, and numbers 1, 2, 3 and 4 had all been chucked out. Willie Weir was one, and the Harbour Master was another one. ..... they tried to put me out and I said, "You can't put me out. ..... I've got six o' a family, so I need a five-bedroomed house," and they told me then that they didnae have a five-bedroomed, which was a lie. They had a five-bedroomed house but there had already been a deal, they had given it to somebody else. ..... [My] family loved the Lammerlaws. It was a beautiful place to live, and no traffic. The only thing that was at the Lammerlaws was a horse and cart, and you couldnae get round the end of our house 'cause there was a big stanchion up in the road, I've still got pictures of it yet.

The Flying Scotsman

Walter Carstairs witnessed the aftermath of the 1914 accident:

..... the next thing I can remember about very clearly was the Flying Scotsman, [which was] going to Aberdeen. And I wakened with a bang. We were living in East Meadows. You know where the East Meadows is? Now, that's going up Cromwell Road, and then on the right hand side, Sandy Blyth had a place in there, Sandy Blyth [had] a garage, what do you call it again, the shop where Dr. Bogie? ..... anyway, one of those doctors. And I ran out, pulling up my trousers and everything, and I ran out, and old Swan came down to back the car out, and he said to me that there had been a train crash on the links, and so the old doctor came down and, of course, got into the car and said, "Do you want a run down, son?" So I jumped in the, well it was a running board in those days. You could stand at the side of the car. So I got my lift down to the Links, and when we arrived there, of course, the thing had happened.

There's many a postcard about it. And all we could see was that the driver and the fireman were killed, 'cause the engine was right into the sand. It had come off the rails, through the rail and then dug itself into the sand. Now it was going some, at that time, it seems, from Edinburgh to Aberdeen. It came in through Burntisland there, nothing to stop it in those days, but this old goods train was backing from the mainline, backing into the opposite side to get out of the road, but it was too late. The Flying Scotsman came around the corner, which is a blind corner there, and struck the [goods train locomotive] and that tilted [the Flying Scotsman's locomotive] over into the sands. ..... well I stayed a while, but I didn't stay very long because the police were there and chased you away, all of us. Now it was ..... 14th [April] 1914 that happened on the Links, the Flying Scotsman came off the line.

*This photograph was taken following the derailment of the Flying Scotsman on 14 April 1914.
It shows the locomotive ('Auld Reekie', number 872), the tender and the first coach, all of
which landed on the Links. Driver Dickson and fireman McDonald were crushed to death
beneath the locomotive, which was partially buried in the soft ground.
J.L. Stevenson collection.*

Another photograph of the railway disaster of 1914. A steam crane begins recovery operations. The railway Roundhouse (engineering workshop) is in the background. J.L. Stevenson collection.

Chapter 7

A Miscellany of Memories

School Days

Jimmy Wilson:

Went to school in Ferguson Place. ..... I went to Pin Robertson, the teacher. Oh, he was a holy terror, he broke my thumb, gave me the belt. I don't know what I had done; I'd done something and I got the belt; got twelve of the belt. And he broke my thumb, and I didn't know it was broken until there was a wee lump began to grow on my wrist and I wondered what it was, and that's what it was, my thumb was broken. And I had to go to an old man, a Mr Watt, who was a railway engine driver, and he was one of these blokes who setted bones up, and repaired things, you know? I'd be 13, something like that, just before I left school, at 14.

He was a bit of a madman. He was mad, Pin Robertson. He used to do awfy daft things, belt dafty. Anyway, I got this belt and I started to play truant, because I wouldna' go to school, and my mother was taken up in front of the school board, and I was in with her, like. Why I wasn't in school, the whys and wherefores of why I didna go to school. And I had to explain to them that I got the belt and my thumb was broken. And I had to ..... get my thumb set ..... they said it would be all right, I never got prosecuted or anything like that.

But I went back to school and I was the best boy in the class. I used to run a' his messages, down the street for his paper and his tobacco and everything like that. I never had any more trouble. I could carry on and do what I liked. But he was, oh, Pin, anybody that was at school wi' me and my age, knew Pin Robertson. I mean, the least thing, ye got the belt. [I left school] when I was 14.

Cherry Rigby:

We had happy days at the school, I must be honest, or did we imagine it? But Pin Robertson, never to be forgotten, never to be forgotten. He was, "Jimmy, if your daughter doesn't get her act together, she'll never, she'll no more pass her qualifying as flying over to Leith." That was his words to my father; never to be forgotten. He was the qualifying [class teacher.] There was him and Mr Wilson. That's why Jean, my friend, we weren't in the same class; she was in Mr Wilson's. That was the posh ones and we were in Pin's. Hard to describe him. Anybody, anybody that's been in Pin's class never forgot it. ..... we thought he was a hard taskmaster, perhaps he wasn't, but we a' thought he was a hard taskmaster.

[We were frightened of him,] and even my daughter, 'cause he was still at the school when Irene was at the school. She was terrified of him before she ever went there. And then, then he retired and it was Mrs Hamilton who took over his class.

[Pin was very generous with] the belt. ..... double-handed, it was always double-handed. One hand on top of the other, yes. ..... you never got one or two from Pin. ..... He had control! I didn't [get the belt.] I don't think so. I don't remember getting it anyway!

[The headmaster in] these days was Pa Rodger.

Burntisland School teachers. BHT collection.
Back row - George Thomson, Miss Peatie, Miss Alice Smith, Miss Brown, Miss Nettie Simpson, Margaret Sutherland, Miss Moss, Mrs Robertson (wife of 'Pin'), Mr Johnson.
Middle row - Miss Toshack, Miss Minn, Mrs Watson, Mrs Sylvia Hollingworth, Mrs Strand, Mr Ramage, Mr Kirkpatrick, 'Sconie' Reid, Isobel Fisher (McCowan), Mrs Lindsay, Miss Inglis, Miss Young.
Front row - Miss Violet Simpson, Mrs McBean, Miss Georgeson, Miss Peggy Aitken, Mr Beattie, Scott Christie (Headmaster), Miss McArthur, 'Pin' Robertson, Miss Annie Gibson, Miss Eva Simpson, Miss McWilliam.

Pin Robertson's class of 1931. Cherry Rigby is in the third row from the back, sixth from the left.
Pin Robertson is on the extreme right. Mr Hendry, the janitor, is on the left of the back row.
Cherry was very conscious of the gender imbalance - 28 boys, but only 14 girls!
Cherry Rigby collection.

Cathie Watson tells of her school days, and of the struggle to make ends meet after her father died:

..... That was Ferguson Place. The same school, the same infant department as it is today and I well remember my first day at school because I had to climb up these steps to the infant's school you see. The same steps that are there today and oh what a job I had getting up. And when I lifted my eyes I saw beautiful feet. Long thin feet and when I raised my eyes there was this beautiful lady. The headmistress! And of course I became a headmistress myself. ..... Looking up to this tall person. Miss Anderson and oh she was delightful and she wore the loveliest shoes and I remember they had about four buttons, criss cross and a strap across here, about four straps across and buttons down the side, and high heels. I was trained on her feet, and then when I looked, my goodness what a beautiful lady, and so beautifully dressed. She took me up to her staff room and asked my name you see, and showed me all the books and things. Looked at the pictures and she asked me questions and then I was taken to the infant room, through a glass partition which is still there to this day, after all those years.

It was a Mr Hamilton-Smith that was the teacher of the qualifying class and the headmaster came round and he said, "Stand all those who want to go to the Higher Grade," and I was quite smart at school. I was near the top and I stood up because I wanted to go to the Higher Grade, to the same buildings that are there today, the very same. And the qualifying teacher said, "Oh yes, Cathie Watson, she's one, third from the top," so that's how I got to the Higher Grade and I was in the Higher Grade till I was 14, you take what you call your Lowers. I was three years in the Higher Grade. That was 12, 13 and 14 and I left Burntisland School when I was 14 and my father was for going on to Kirkcaldy High School, and the headmaster said, "Oh no, no, it's disreputed just now, I'm sending you all to Dunfermline High School."

..... I was only 15 when daddy departed. He wasn't ill at all. He just took a pain and it was a burst appendix. A matter of hours. I finished with Burntisland School in July of 1915. I finished school in July and in six weeks he had died. And there was I and mother, and I was to go to Dunfermline High School and no money. Nothing, nothing. In those days we didn't get anything. She wasn't old enough. She wanted to get an old age pension. ..... oh dear we had a terrible struggle. However she said, "Your father wanted you to go on and so we'll see what we can do." So we had this big house in Greenmount Road. So she took in boarders and we had one boarder ..... The district nurse, Nurse Neilson. Neilson Grove is called after her and she was the District Nurse and lived with us in this big house in Greenmount Road, where the Christies live now. Well that was my home for 40 years and we wondered what we would do when daddy died of course, and she took in the District Nurse for a place to live.

She was six years with us. A pound a week and that kept us going. And of course I had a little brother. I wasn't just alone. A pound a week from Nurse Neilson and she had the downstairs bedroom to herself and she paid for her lunch which was a shilling. There was a nursing association in those days and they used to come and have their monthly meetings in our house in our front sitting room. Nurse Neilson was very happy with us until they bought a house for her eventually. The Nursing Association collected a lot of money and asked people to contribute towards it and had sales of work and all the rest of it. They bought a house in the Crescent. You know where the Inchview Hotel is? Well it was just about there. A flat, and we used to go and see her and have tea with her. She was a lovely sweet person. She was born and brought up in Edinburgh, down Leith, Leith Walk somewhere.

I remember going once with the District Nurse on the milk cart. There was a baby to be born at one of the farms. She had to go up to this birth you see, and I went with her because I didn't want her to go out alone you see, and we sat side by side with the driver behind this horse, all the way up to this farm way up the back of the Binn, and we weren't home till about four in

141

the morning. I couldn't bear the thought of my wee nurse going away on her own and she was glad of the company of course but that was quite an experience.

..... our school in Ferguson Place took fire, 1911 or 1914[1]. The Middle School took fire. I remember standing. We were all told to go out into the street and I remember standing in Ferguson Place and looking up at our class. It was before the war and they were blaming the Germans for setting fire to it! ..... all our books were burned and everything and we had to start in the Leven Street Hall and, oh, I objected to this. I had to walk across the Links every day, away to the Leven Street Hall and we had no books or anything. So they bought, penny, what do you call them, penny books or something, there is a name they have. I remember reading 'The Charcoal Burner'! Very apt! And the Leven Street Hall was so hard to sit on. You were just sitting on a step. Horrible seats after our nice desks. They were all burnt.

Above - Burntisland School on fire in 1913. Below left - Nurse Neilson. Alan Barker and BHT collections.

Violet McFarlane:

We lived in a small house, owned by the Miss Aitkens, [at] the bottom before you go up to Braehead, ... not a cul-de-sac, just about four houses down there. Then we moved up to the centre of the Kirkton. I started school, I can't remember the first day, but I can remember walking through the drill hall to get to my class. But there were two doors in the drill hall, and the two Miss Shands, were sisters I presume, one was in the one door and one in the other. Then when you went through the door that I did go through, there was Miss Thomson on the one side door and Mrs McKenzie on the other. And then later on it was upstairs and I sat beside my lifelong friend, of over sixty years, never losing contact,

---

[1] Actually March 1913.

Jessie Dick, her own name. And then I moved on to Mr Robertson's class – and he was a worthy!

The Town Council

Burntisland Town Council was wound up when local government was reorganised in 1975.

Isa Duncanson:

I was always interested in the Council ..... there was an association formed, called the Civic Association, non-political, 'cause I wouldn't have had, ever, anything to do with politics and this was the Civic Association, and it was started up. And there was someone from there said to me, "Would you not be interested in standing for the Town Council, because you do such a lot for the town?" At first, I thought, no, I don't think I would like that at all. And then, other people were saying to me, "Why don't you stand for the Town Council?" So I did it, I did it and Jack was on the Town Council, my husband, but I hadn't even met Jack at that time. So he was one of the candidates as well, and there was Donald Gavin, and there was Tom Hynes, Stewart Marshall, and Frank Lovern, who was the harbour master at the time, lived at the Lammerlaws.

So we had this Civic Association. So, stood for the Council, and, I think, from what I can remember, I think Jack and I were first and second, at the top of the polls ..... And quite a few of us got in, Donald Gavin and, I can't remember, I think it was Stewart Marshall got in, and that was the first time, really, that they had broken a political council, you know. So quite enjoyed that and then, when it came the next election, the Civic Association candidates actually, they then had control of the Council, I think we were ten-two. .....

I always objected to, the parties would have a meeting before the Council meeting, as I suppose that they still do yet, even in Parliament, and they did all the decisions of what they were going to vote for and everything. And I can always remember being quite tickled about this because there was a lady councillor, and she always used to sit next to me in the Burgh Chambers, and something would come up, and she would say, "Oh, I don't approve of that. Oh, no, no, I don't approve of that." But when the vote came, she voted for it, you see. And I could never have done that. You know, I had the courage of my own convictions. That was one wee thing that I didn't quite like about it.

But on the whole, they were happy years as well on the Town Council. We did quite a lot. I was at one point the Health and Cleansing Convener, which I liked, that was quite good. And Jack was the Housing Convener. That was a nuisance, because you never sat down to a meal but somebody came to your house, wondering when they were going to get a house. Council houses, you see. .....

That's what's wrong today, because when you had your own Town Council, everybody knew somebody who they could go to if there was something that they needed or they wanted to know about. Now, your council's faceless, in a way.

..... they had what they called the Public Gallery at the back ..... there was certain meetings the public didn't get into, but you had the big Council meeting on the first Monday of the month. But then ..... you had small meetings with your own sub-committee ..... there was a committee with a convener, see, so maybe four Council members on, say, onto my committee, the Health and Cleansing. You'd four members plus the Burgh Surveyor.

Then if it was anything to do with the financial business, the Burgh Chamberlain was there, for he handled the finance. Then you'd to go to conferences, and I always quite enjoyed that, they were interesting. Opened your eyes, ... there would be councillors there - not our councillors, 'cause I was the representative who went from here - and Albert Watson [the Burgh Surveyor] always, he usually went with me. But there were other councillors from little towns

Burntisland Town Council in July 1969. BHT collection.
Left to right at the rear table - Bailie Miss J.M. Simpson, Mr Hugh Cameron (Town Officer), Provost John
A. Duncanson, Police Judge Donald F. Gavin, Bailie A.B. Allan, Mr A.C. Watson (Burgh Surveyor).
Left to right round the main table - Councillor Mrs Isa Duncanson, Councillor T. Allan, Councillor S. Bolam, Dean
of Guild George Gunn, Mr G. Beagrie (Assistant Burgh Surveyor), Mr H. Robertson (Assistant in the Burgh
Chamberlain's Department), Mr. W. Leslie Stewart (Burgh Chamberlain), Mr George Maclachlan (Town Clerk),
Honorary Treasurer Stewart Marshall, Councillor F. Lovern, Councillor W. Baillie, Councillor R.M. Livingstone.

not far from here and they never attended a session of the conference. ..... all the housing people, like Wimpey and all these people, they all took a suite in a hotel and they entertained from morning until night, you see, wanting the council to give them the order to build houses ..... they never came, just used to copy somebody's notes. That's right. I always thought it was terrible, when I saw people doing that ..... I thought, gosh, fancy going to a conference and you don't even go to the conference. But that was what happened, so it opened your eyes. But, no, I enjoyed that. Went to one at Rothesay and Inverness, Carnoustie, 'cause Jane, my daughter, she was only about six weeks old when I went to the one at Carnoustie and what we used to do was, there was a friend of mine, and Jack used to pay for this friend for to go with me and she used to look after the child, you see, that was how we worked it. But it was good; it was really good.

Yes, I was [still a Councillor when my husband, Jack, was elected Provost.] ..... I had William, the second child, ... during his term of office. 'Cause I remember when I was in Forth Park and there was Charlotte Haddow, and other councillors all called. ..... it was the first time it had ever happened to a Provost's wife, had given birth to a son during his term of office. So there you go. I said to William, "You're a very important baby, you know!" ..... so I was on for part of Jack's term. I think Jack did four years [as Provost,] if I remember, but then I think I didn't stand, I think I finished my term, which was three years, and I didn't stand again when I came to have the second child.

..... you'd twelve councillors, it was always twelve, and every year, four came off. So there was four seats vacant every year. ..... every council had its own local election, which I used to work at years before I was on the Council. And what you did then, was, you worked all day at the voting and then you'd to count them at night, and it was all done in the school gym, up there.

..... going years back, when you look at really old photographs of the Town Council, it was all the businessmen of the Town that were on your Council. ..... it was businessmen that were sort of running your town, ... financially, they were quite good at advising and things like that.

..... The next level was the County Council in Cupar. 'Cause Jack used to go to meetings. He was appointed to that, and I think it was mainly like your provost - your head of Council - and maybe your bailies, they would have to attend County Council meetings, you see. That was the next level. That was all; you used to have the Town Council and the County Council. And they dealt with things that the Council didn't deal with. And then of course, they started all this regionalisation, which funnily enough, Jack was very, very against ..... And I remember, he was so against it, and I said, "But why? Why are you fighting this and what for?" and he said, "I'll tell you why, because in twenty years time, Burntisland'll be a shanty town." And for a while, it's looking better now, but for a while, when you looked on the High Street and you thought you were right. He said, "All the little towns'll just become shanty towns and everything'll be for Kirkcaldy and Glenrothes." And that's really what happens, mostly.

..... [You could go to the Burgh Yard] and say, "..... I've got a drippy pipe," or, "I've got a leak," or something, and they just took it from there and they did it. It's all so different now.

..... everybody knew who swept the roads, and if he hadn't swept it right, he would have been in trouble. Which is true, though. They'd have said, "Oh, that Jock Smith," or whoever it is, "isn't sweeping, you know. He goes and stands in a corner." But now people don't even know who to complain to. It's very, very different.

..... She was a Labour Councillor, Miss [Daisy] McRae, and her father before her had been on the Council. That'll be going back a long, long way. ..... She lived to almost a hundred if she wasn't a hundred, and she was in Allan Court. ..... she [had] lived in Broomhill Avenue with her father, and father had been a bailie, I think, as well, and then she was a bailie.

And then the other ..... lady, when I was on the Council, was Miss Simpson, Miss Nettie Simpson, and she was a bailie. So was Donald Gavin, he was a bailie.

..... I'll tell you another thing the Council used to do, you had the waterworks outing, once a year. ..... Oh, a great day, the waterworks outing. ..... Oh yes, it was a big day and the private bus, you all met at the Town Hall and then you went from the Town Hall up to the waterworks, to the reservoir [at Stenhouse.] You were inspecting the reservoir. ..... So you did that and the person in charge up at the reservoir, he showed you all the workings and everybody looked to see. You did that and then you got all in the bus and then you went away somewhere and you stopped ..... to have your coffee, and you went on again on a lovely drive and stopped off for a meal, and they all come home at night. But in the olden days, we were told, when they went on the waterworks outing, they went away and then by the time they all came home at night, they were all so fu' .....

..... the Burgh Chamberlain, him and his staff, they handled all the finance. And then of course, the Town Clerk, you had a Town Clerk who handled all the legal matters, and that was George Maclachlan for years and years and years. And we were on the Council when they appointed the new Town Clerk, who was Mrs Hadden. And unfortunately, Mrs Hadden didn't live all that long here. ..... she was very good, and that was the first time there had been a lady Town Clerk, of course. But, no, she was very, very good, very good. But it was George Maclachlan for years and years and years. And then I think, after George finished up, I think George Pollock [of Brown & Gilmour] did it for a little while. .....

An old aerial view of Burntisland.
Alan Barker collection.

The junction of Cromwell Road, Buccleuch Place, High Street and Rose Street,
showing an early overtaking manoeuvre.
Alan Barker collection.

That's another position that we had on the Town Council, was the Treasurer, you had an Honorary Treasurer. ..... it was just really in name, and he would have to do all his conferring with the Burgh Chamberlain. But that was really your, that's where all your money was handled, there.

The Local Police and the Burgh Court

Jim Cowie:

Well, in 1963, when I came here, ... in fact when I joined the police in 1961, it was still run very much on traditional lines. In Kirkcaldy, it was still run on the old Burgh Police lines. You paraded, you quick marched out the door and you went off to your respective foot beats. That was the system in the burghs until 1949. Fife, in fact, had three police forces: Fife County, Kirkcaldy Burgh and Dunfermline City, and they amalgamated to form the force as it is now. So, in Burntisland, it was still run on traditional lines, as a small county station. It was, in fact, a sub-division, with an inspector, two sergeants in Burntisland and a sergeant in Inverkeithing, and covered an area from the outskirts of Kirkcaldy to North Queensferry, at that time.

In Burntisland, the inspector, two sergeants, nine constables. Kinghorn had two constables, Aberdour, two, Inverkeithing, a sergeant and perhaps four, I think, and one in North Queensferry.

..... The town closed down about ten o'clock, the licensed premises closed at that time and everyone went home. Except for activity round at the docks when there was ships in, of course. Well, there was always an attraction for [certain] females in the town; the ladies of the night, as they were known. ..... But it was all on a, sort of, well-known, friendly basis, actually. We knew, they knew, and I've used this term before, but they were all enthusiastic amateurs!

..... Well, to take you through, first of all, the [court] procedure, particularly at any court, whether it's a cited court or a custody court, was to meet, first of all, in the adjacent Magistrates' Room [here in the Burgh Chambers], and round the table there, sat the Magistrate, the Bailie; the Clerk of the Court; local solicitor; the Burgh Prosecutor, William Strang; Duncan, the solicitor from, I think it was about Leslie he came [from]; the police officer who was there because we prepared all the summonses and the citations and they were all prepared in the police station in Burntisland. That was part of our role, and, of course, in the corner, stood the Burgh Officer, and he was resplendent in his uniform ..... Hugh Cameron, that's right, Hugh Cameron. So we would be seated round the table, the summons would be laid out, and, "Oh, yes, what have we got today then?" "So-and-so, so-and-so and so-and-so."

..... In fact the original [Burntisland] police station is in the building that we're in now[2], to the rear. That was built in the 1800s, until the new police station was built on Links Place. A new Burgh Court was built there, and, in the fashion of the time, the police station and the Burgh Court were usually in the same building. The old police station in Links Place, which was the one my father served at, has the old Burgh Court, three cells, they're still there. That's where the Air Cadets are now. The usual front office, sergeant's room, inspector's room .....

..... the new one was built in the 1950s, on the High Street. It was much the same, three cells, various muster rooms, sergeant's room, front office, inspector's room, kitchen, etc.

[The Links Place building] certainly is [a bit of antiquity.] It's ..... terrific. [I've] often felt it's a great focal point for a museum, or sub like.

..... we can all, all of us who were stationed here can relate, at some time or another, to some incident. But one does stick out in my mind. On a rare occasion when there was a trial, it

---

[2] The Burgh Chambers.

was a local lady; she was a wee bit notorious, and given to disturb the peace occasionally. And she'd had problems with a boyfriend, and alleged she'd been assaulted by him, and it went to trial. So ..... her solicitor was taking her through the account of it and then asked, "So, Miss so-and-so, the accused struck you?" "That's right." "And what did you do?" "Well I just turned roond and effing punched 'im, because he wisnae gonna do that to me." End of trial! .....

Well I think the most disturbing [incidents] would be where it were a death, industrial or accidental, particularly on the railways. ..... the shipyard, unfortunately, there were deaths there as well. And in the Alcan, not often, but I do remember going to one, one night, in the aluminium works. It was a local chap, who'd gone through the conveyor system, and he looked intact, but every bone in his body was shattered.

Isa Duncanson:

..... there were bailies, the bailies who sat on the court in Burntisland. There's a courtroom up in the Burgh Chambers, and that was the courtroom, and there was three bailies appointed; a Provost and three bailies. And the court met once every week, I think it was.

..... I remember the first one that Jack sat on as Provost, and I think the court sat, I think a Thursday, that rings a bell, and he come home a bit put out because this old man had thrown a brick through the police station window, and of course, he was up the next morning, you see, at the court in front of Jack. And he said it was awful, it was awful, 'cause he kept saying, "Please, your Lordship, just put me inside. I've nowhere to stay. Would you just please put me inside, your Lordship?" And Jack thought this was terrible, terrible. An old man who'd nowhere to live, so he threw a brick through the window, to get arrested and get put inside .....

The Buses

Walter Carstairs:

..... travel in these days would be difficult. Buses ran from the old picture house[3] that I'm talking about ..... they used to go to the back of the [picture house,] they'd go [and get] the gas first, and they filled up with gas ..... big balloons on top of them ..... gas was pumped into them ..... and they drove from Burntisland to Kinghorn, to Kirkcaldy. They didn't go into Kirkcaldy, they only went as far as the Links ..... and turned there and went back again to Burntisland, and fivepence, I can remember that. It was thruppence to Kinghorn and thruppence from Kinghorn to Kirkcaldy. If you took the through ticket, it was fivepence.

The Early Days of Motoring

Jim Harvey:

I always remember, the first Saturday after I got my car, I took my wife into Kirkcaldy, and the whole of the Esplanade in Kirkcaldy, there was only one car there, and it belonged to Mr Maclachlan, the lawyer here. So that's how things have changed in Kirkcaldy, since I got my first car.

I learned to drive in Edinburgh. When I was in business I had a whole lot of travellers coming in, and this day the ironmonger's traveller, who I got on very well with. I says, "I'm wanting to learn to drive. Could you recommend a ..... driving school in Edinburgh?" "Well," he says, "there's one that advertises their passes every month. They're called the Castle School of

---

[3] The Porte Cinema.

Motoring. It's in Castle Street." So I went there, and that's where I learned to drive. I wanted to learn in the traffic, no' the likes o' Burntisland, where there wasn't much traffic. I wanted to learn in the city, so that being in heavy traffic ..... wouldn't trouble me. And that's what I did. And fortunately I was able to get through ..... After my first eight lessons, I passed. So I was quite pleased at that.

Alterations to the Parish Church

Jim Harvey:

I think one o' the main things that I got greatest pleasure out of, all the time that I've been in business, was in 1962, when Jim Monaghan was a minister here. He had read over the history o' the church, and before that time, Mr Orr was very keen on doing certain alterations to the church, which we couldn't afford.

He came to me and he said, "I think if we put our heads together, Jim, we could come up with something simpler which would do the same thing," and this is what we did. So the church as it is just now, the alterations that took place at that time was quite a lot.

Well, just prior to that, the organ had been shifted from the vestry door to the centre o' the church, and the choir sat round about that. But they felt they wanted the organ [moved,] to open the choir range out to the congregation. So this was done, and the choir range extended to a certain extent. The organ was put up. We formed a choir gallery and a west gallery. At that time, the north gallery panels were different from all the rest, due to a fire, which had taken place in the church, several years before. And there was certain panels on it, before it was destroyed. And for a period of time, they were put in a picture hanging on the wall. Now, eventually, due to money which was given to us by the late Session Clerk, Charlie Dallas. He gave us money to replace the front of that gallery, and that was replaced the same as what the rest of it was. That work was done wi' a firm in Edinburgh.

This was 1962 that it was restored to what it was. The church was completely redecorated; the vestibule modernised. The church was completely rewired, and it was quite an event, the opening of the church, after that. That was one occasion when the church was absolutely full, it was. It was a great night.

Catholic Church Services

Betty Traynor:

When we first came to the town there were very few Catholics and we didn't have a church so the service was held in a house at the bottom of Somerville Street and the Priest came along from Kirkcaldy when he could manage. Later on, of course, the church was along Kinghorn Road next to the Sands Hotel and the Priest lived up at the Coastguard's house above the Church Hall.

Surgery on the Kitchen Table

Norman Mackie: As a schoolboy we were brought up in Lesslie's Buildings in the Kirkton across the road and apparently my tonsils had been affected by something. The doctor who was Dr King decided to do the operation at home instead of sending me to a hospital. So Nurse Neilson was the local nurse, where we have a street called after her, so Dr King and Nurse

Neilson, I was laid out on the kitchen table, and operated on, and when I come to, one thing I did want was an ice cream, and that's all I can remember about my operation. My throat was sore but I was all right after I had the ice cream! My tonsils were taken out on a kitchen table. I was just seven because I was at school and that was to save going into hospital, a brave boy was he. ..... it was a mask they put over but it wasnt an up to date way of putting you out to sleep!

The Roundhouse Bell

Norman Mackie:

I've been very fortunate I've had a wonderful memory of noises. Sounds in the town. One was the Roundhouse bell, or the 'Roondhoose' bell. A few years ago I was walking round by where the Roundhouse was and I thought I think I'll write a few words about the Roundhouse bell. It was rung each morning at half past seven for the men to come to their work at eight o'clock. So I wrote these few words:

The Roondhoose Bell

The hurry and scurry o' trampin' feet
Nae longer heard doon Union Street
When the tollin' o' the Roondhoose bell
Summoned a' the loons frae dock and dell.
Although ye travelled far awa
And missed the bonny Lammerlaw,
Ye'll aye think back wi' pride an' dwell
As ye hear in the distance the Roondhoose bell.

The Salmon Nets

Cathie Watson:

I remember the salmon nets [at Pettycur Sands,] we used to paddle out there. I never saw any salmon in them. Yes, they were there before the war[4] and then when the war broke out they were frightened for aeroplanes landing so they put lots of other posts but the ones for salmon had nets between them you see, to catch the salmon. I don't know if there is still salmon in the Forth.

Andrew Young

Cathie Watson:

..... Oh yes, yes, [Andrew Young was] a very great friend [of my father.] That's why I have these pictures ..... painted by him. He was an artist, and a photographer as well, and wrote as well, a most talented man. And he had the funniest old fashioned wife you ever saw. ..... he painted the most wonderful picture which was bought by America unfortunately, Fair, have you

---

[4] The First World War.

not heard of it? ..... It was [used for] a calendar. Mr Thomson the grocer, he chose it as a calendar one year and people got that for their Xmas from Thomson the Grocer. ..... so we just cut them out and got them framed at once of course, because my father was so fond of that. You see they just lived round the corner from us. Young lived opposite the Orcadia on the railway side. ..... the very first one on the corner. ..... he took a photograph of daddy in a kilt here, ... dressed as a Highlander with a kilt and thick stockings and a tweed jacket and painted a picture of it.

The Orcadia

[The Orcadia[5]] was a girl's school, that's right. A Mr Davidson bought it ..... now do I know any girls that were at the school, no I don't think so. It was a private school. A Mr Davidson bought it. There was a big firm of motor engineers about the 1920s, Biggar, Fleming and Davidson, three men, and they formed this company, they had cars and they sold cars and they had a shop ..... at the bottom of the Kirkgate, their shop was there and they sold bicycles and motor cars. You could hire a car there if you wanted to go anywhere.

[The school was for girls] who had wealthy parents. I didn't know any of them that were there. I had no idea. And sometimes people who were going abroad would leave their family here so they might stay in. Could be a boarding school. Can't really remember that very well. There was a big high wall round it you see. You never got in to see what it was like. Very private. It was made into a nursing home at one time and I got in then and I noticed that it had French windows. I was surprised when I got through this gate because there was just this wee door in the wall and it was always shut.

Life in Buccleuch Place

Cherry Rigby:

I was born at 2 Buccleuch Place, which is right next to the War Memorial. I was born on a Sunday, the sun was shining and the silver band was playing on the Links; my mother told me that. [Our house] was one bedroom and a kitchen. It had an earth floor and a pig-iron sink; horrible pig-iron sink. But we did have an inside toilet to ourselves, which was a great thing in those days. We had linoleum that covered the earth floor. Very basic, but we lived on the Links.

..... my Mum had to do all her washing along at my grandmother's washhouse, at the cottage. I don't know what they would have done if it hadn't been for my grandmother's washhouse.

..... if you wanted a bath, you had to go along to the washhouse to have a bath, and stoke the boiler up and get the hot water that way, definitely. But that was a great thing, when I think about it, that was a great washhouse, because we used to stay there in the summer and let the house [in Buccleuch Place], let our house ..... I loved sleeping in the washhouse!

The Links

Cherry Rigby:

..... Yes, the cattle grazed on the Links. They came down from the Kirkton Dairy. It was

---

[5] Now the Burntisland Sands Hotel.

along Aberdour Road? They grazed there and I think it was a farmer called Brown that had those, and they *did* [graze there.] They used [the Links] for what it was intended. ..... never, never seemed to bother about the washing [that was hung out on the Links].

The Public Baths

Cherry Rigby:

[If we couldn't get into the washhouse,] we had to go to the baths at the Lochies. Sixpence for a bath and you got your soap and your towel. There was no stipulation, no shortage o' the time. [They heated the water] with the wood that was brought up from the beach. There was a tremendous amount of driftwood, 'cause my Grandfather had a little business going with his wood! He used to dry the wood round the fire, then chop it up for kindling and it was a penny a bunch!

Cathie Watson:

..... Oh yes, and not only people who didn't have a bath in their house went down for a bath. Public baths. They paid for it. I think it was a shilling a bath. ..... if they had no bath in the house, lots of houses without baths.

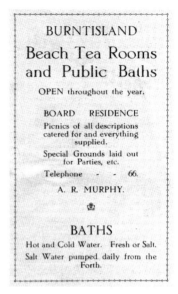

An old advertisement.
BHT collection.

Old Names

Cherry Rigby:

[We called the cemetery] Tam Chalmers's. That's Tam Chalmers's, we always spoke about going to Tam Chalmers's. Because he looked after the cemetery .....
..... we never called the Erskine Church [clock anything other than] the 'Glory to God'. Miss Macomish donated it and that's what's [inscribed] on it.

Rossend Castle

Walter Carstairs:

We got married in the castle, '33, 1933. I got married by Dabb in the castle. Aye. The Reverend Dabb. He married me in the castle. ..... Aye, well that big, big room in the middle of it is still where all the functions were held. That was where the weddings were held. And the ladies used to put their clothes in the famous bedroom that Mary, Queen of Scots [used.]

Cathie Watson:

Oh yes, I remember [the Castle as a hotel.] I used to go there for dancing lessons. Madge MacArthur who lived in Nether Grange and she taught dancing. So we had all the different steps. We had the Highland fling, the six steps of the Highland Fling and we had ballroom dancing. How to waltz, how to foxtrot. There is a beautiful drawing room there at Rossend Castle. I haven't seen it for years but it had cushioned seats all around about it, especially round the windows, you know. Oh it was a lovely room. It was upstairs.

Rossend Castle. Alan Barker collection.

The gateway to Rossend Castle. The small lodge on the left with the lattice window was the home of Burntisland School Headmaster, Pa Rodger. As Cherry Rigby relates, the lodge was demolished to allow better access to the Castle area. Alan Barker collection.

Violet McFarlane:

I went to work in the Castle as a house table-maid. Rossend Castle, I should say it that way. Rossend Castle was a private boarding house at that time, not a bed and breakfast. Quite a few people came from Edinburgh to stay there every year. They came on holiday. It was just a place for people who had money to come over and spend a week there. I can still see that dining room, very much so.

Cherry Rigby:

Pa Rodger [was the headmaster] and he stayed at the Castle. Lodged at the Castle, yes, and I loved their little lodge. I thought it was a lovely little lodge that was at the gate of the Castle. And they had to knock it down, because people couldn't get to the houses at the Castle wi' their furniture. That's one o' the reasons it had to come down, the access.

Top - an advertisement for Rossend Castle guest house. BHT collection.
Main picture - Rossend Castle on the verge of demolition. Alan Barker collection.

Isa Duncanson recalls the battle to save Rossend Castle, which was led by her husband Jack and which lasted from 1962 to 1975:

..... that was quite a saga, that, because the Labour councillors at that time, they wanted it demolished, and Jack, he fought and fought for it to be kept. And I can remember very heated Council meetings. Even a Councillor saying to Jack, "If you want to save this castle, save it with your own money." Well that was uncalled for, but, oh there was a lot of stooshies over that, really, it was awful. And we were sitting in the house one afternoon, when the phone rang, and it was an old lady who lived opposite the Castle, a Mrs Rae, and she was calling to speak to Jack to say the bulldozer had arrived to knock it down. And Jack, right away, phoned Wheeler & Sproson [architects], who'd always been fighting, wanting to keep the Castle as well. So he phoned, and either Mr Wheeler or Sproson, I don't know which one it would be, was to meet him up [there,] and he stopped it. He stopped them knocking it down, but it was as near as that to being knocked down. .....

Jack Duncanson. Isa Duncanson collection.

And the ..... Councillor who wanted it knocked down - who was there welcoming all the guests on the day when it was re-opened? It was him, and as one lady said to me, she said, "I could hardly look at him, because I know he wanted it knocked down," and unfortunately, Jack had passed away before it all happened. He never saw it.

..... for months and months we just ate and slept Rossend Castle. It was as strong as that. He was so determined it wouldn't be knocked down. ..... Any time I've been to cheese and wines and whatnot there, I always think, Jack, you would have been quite proud of this .....